A History of Angel Grove Baptist Church

Book One
1888-1988

This book was originally published by Angel Grove Baptist Church in 1988, to celebrate the 100th anniversary of our Church.

We have taken great care to recreate it as it was, with as little editing as possible.

Some pictures may be crooked, some text may be a bit blurred, but this was the the technology of the day.

We hope you find it as wonderful as we have!

Table of Contents

History
Of
Angel Grove
Baptist Church

1888 - 1988

DEDICATION

This book is dedicated to God our Father, the Maker and Creator of all things and for His honor and glory. To Jesus Christ our Lord who shed his blood for us all. To the Holy Spirit who dwells within us. To the memory of the sixteen men and women who came together in 1888 to establish this local body of believers in Jesus Christ, known as the Angel Grove Baptist Church. To all past, present, and future members, without whom this local body could not exist. To all Pastors who have served, are serving, or will serve as Shepherd of this body. And last, to everyone who has had a part in making the publishing of this book possible.

HISTORICAL COMMITTEE

Will S. Prickett	Becky Craven	Curtis Johnson
Geraldine Prickett	Lawrence Burgess	Pat Miller
Anita Burns	Dora Sue Angel	Tracy Pritchett
Joyce Tillison		

Rev. Eugene Burgess

On August 11, 1888, under the leadership of Rev. H. L. Johnson of Weaver Station and Rev. G.S. Boozer of Ohatchee, sixteen "professors of faith in this community" gathered together to establish a new church. The seven men and nine women were examined by a presbytery of Brothers J.C. Cross, Tiler Henderson, and George Brittain of Post Oak Springs. When the petitioning members were found to be "one in Christ," they were constituted to join a church by the name of Angel Grove. The petitioning members who were examined were Brothers J.M. Propes, D.B. Johnson, J.W. Propes, J.R. Johnson, A.D. Powell, Robert Willingham, and Jesse Willingham, along with Sisters Rose Propes, Nannie Angel, Jane Snider, M.J. Johnson, Sara Propes, Samanthy Lucads, M.A. Johnson, Pernacy Lanford, and Mattie Lanford.

The original church building itself was located in a grove of trees on a plot of land donated to the church's membership January 3, 1890, by R.J. (Jeff) Angel and his wife Nannie -- thus, the church was named Angel Grove.

Jeff Angel had come to the area, then known as Tampa, from Cherokee County when he was twelve years old. His mother, a widow, married William Woodley and brought her son to live in Tampa. Jeff Angel grew and married Nannie Anderson at the age of 19. Together they reared five sons and two daughters who continued to live in the area, as did most of their own children.

For decades his descendants owned most of the land -- a situation which caused the area to remain primarily rural in character. In the early 1900's Tampa was primarily an agricultural area. Cotton, corn, and grain were raised, as were cattle.

The East and West Railroad Line once served the community. There was a large wooden water tank beside the East and West tracks. The steam locomotives stopped to take on water for their boilers. Jeff Angel was in charge of the tank, pumping water from Buck Creek into the elevated tank. The Seaboard Coastline Railroad bought out East and West and moved the tracks a short distance. At the time of the move the community had already lost its Tampa post office, so Seaboard renamed its depot Angel Station to honor the man who operated the water tank.

The large tank that services the locomotives traveling the Seaboard tracks was no longer needed when diesel engines replaced the steam powered ones, so the depot was eventually phased out of use.

A cluster of businesses formed around the station. A general store was operated by Tom Moore. Two sons of Jeff Angel, Will and Tom, operated a cotton gin and oil mill. There was a sawmill, a dry kiln, and a planing mill located nearby. Cotton warehouses were eventually constructed to store surplus government cotton.

As the community continued to grow, so did its church. Because of the agricultural interests of its members, Angel Grove was like many rural churches in the 1920's and '30's. Since it was sometimes necessary for church members to move from place to place to find work, these churches had a very transient membership. Angel Grove lost members to and obtained members from neighboring churches. The members sometimes donated a portion of their crop to the church when money was scarce.

The annual summer protracting meetings which began each 4th Sunday in July often added 20 to 30 members to the church roll. On the Sunday following each week of meetings, a baptismal service was held at the creek beside the home of Jim and Addie Angel. The Angels opened their home to supply a place for the baptismal candidates to change clothes before returning to the church for regular morning services.

Rev. G.S. Morris annually held an evangelist's meeting at Cedar Springs schoolhouse located about 3 miles from the church. Angel Grove and other churches neighboring the school "opened the doors" to members who wished to join through Rev. Morris's services.

The fellowship of the church has been manifested through its "love offering" for members in need and its dedicated prayer services. The growth has also been fun -- with annual picnics, all-day singings, special Christmas traditions, and youth retreats.

The progress of the church and the concern of its membership are evident reasons that Angel Grove Baptist Church has continued to grow for 100 years. Although the earliest records prior to 1920 have been destroyed or misplaced, the existing minutes reveal a concern for growing numbers and an attempt to provide the best facilities and ministries possible. The following entries are actual excerpts from the church minutes. Because of the very personal nature of some entries, some of the names have been deleted; other entries have been condensed or paraphrased. Quotation marks have been inserted to show exact words taken from the minutes. Spelling and grammatical errors have been corrected. Explanations are in parenthesis.

The church was in the Tallahassee Ten Island Association from 1888 until 1882, when it joined the newly organized Calhoun County Baptist Association. Angel Grove's first delegates to the associational meeting were D. B. Johnson, William Turk, and Pastor H. L. Johnston, who represented the church's 31 members.

In May of 1915 the nearby Seven Springs Cemetery was deeded to Angel Grove Church by Dave and Kate Cowden. The members of local churches organized the annual cleaning and decoration of the graves by hosting a "dinner on the grounds" and memorial service on the Saturday before each 4th Sunday in May.

The State of Alabama,
Calhoun County.

This Indenture made and entered into this the 3rd day of January 1890 by and between R. J. Angel & wife Nannie E. Angel

of the first part, and J. N. Propst & N. P. Turk Deacons of Angel Grove Baptist Church and their Successors in Office

of the second part, witnesseth that the said party of the first part, for and in consideration of the sum of One Dollars

to them in hand paid, the receipt whereof is hereby acknowledged, ~~and promissory notes recorded by the said part of the second part, bearing even date with this instrument, and due and payable as follows:~~

The Said lot of land to be Controlled by the Officers & members of Said Church and a School building to be located thereon for the Education of Children

hath granted, bargained, sold and conveyed, and do by these presents, grant, bargain, sell and convey unto the said party of the second part, and unto their Successors in office forever, the following described real estate, viz: to be used exclusively for the Said Baptist church and School purpose described as follows — Beginning where the west boundary line of the Section crosses the Jacksonville and Gadsden Public Road. thence East with Center of Said Road Two hundred & Seventy (270) feet thence South one hundred & sixty one and one third (161⅓) feet; thence West two hundred & Seventy (270) feet to the west line of the Section — thence forth on Said Section line one hundred & Sixty one and one third (161⅓) feet to the point of beginning. Containing One acre in the West half of the NW¼ Section Six, T 14, S R 8 E

situated in Calhoun County, Alabama, with all the tenements and appurtenances thereunto belonging, or in anywise appertaining.

To Have and to Hold to the said party of the second part, their ~~heirs and assigns~~ Successors in Office forever. And the said party of the first part, for themselves, their heirs, executors and administrators will forever warrant and defend the title of the above bargained premises against the claims of all persons whatsoever.

In testimony whereof the aforesaid party of the first part have hereunto set our hands and seals the day and year above written.

Witness :

R. J. Angel (L.S.)
Nannie Angel (L.S.)

10

Jeff Angel came to the area known as Tampa with his mother when he was only twelve years old. He later married Nannie Anderson. Together they reared five sons and two daughters. They donated the land where the original church building was built.

Mr. & Mrs. Robert Jefferson Angel

Mrs. Nannie Angel (Last Charter Member to die - 1936)
Her childred Maggie Wynn, Elizabeth Weaver, Walt, Jim, Will, Tom and Edd Angel

A sketch of the old church building which was located in a grove of trees just below the site of the present church. The sketch was drawn by Mrs. Kathryn Putman.

STATE OF ALABAMA)
)
CALHOUN COUNTY   )

KNOW ALL MEN BY THESE PRESENTS: That for and in consideration

of the sum of   Ten and no/100 ($10.00)------------------------

Dollars, and other valuable consideration in hand paid, to the under-

signed by   ANGEL GROVE BAPTIST CHURCH

the receipt of which is hereby acknowledged, we   the undersigned

grant ors,   G. W. ANGEL and his wife, DORIS P. ANGEL

ha ve this day bargained and sold, and by these presents do   hereby

grant, bargain, sell and convey unto   ANGEL GROVE BAPTIST CHURCH

the following described tract or parcel of land, lying and being in

Calhoun County, Alabama, and more particularly bounded and described

as follows:

> 2.01 acres in Section 1, Township 14 South, Range 7 East and
> Section 6, Township 14 South, Range 8 East described as be-
> ginning at the junction of the East line of Section 1 and the
> South line of Alabama Highway No. 204. Said Junction being
> 1535.6 feet South of the Northeast corner of Section 1, thence
> North 51 degrees and 57 minutes West along the South line of
> said Highway 90.9 feet, thence South 33 degrees and 58 min.West
> 298.1 ft.,thence South 13 degrees and 22 min.East 158.7 ft.,thence
> South 45 degrees and 29 min.East 174.3 ft.,thence South 74 degrees
> and 51 min.East 136.0 ft.,thence North 24 degrees and 50 min.East
> 54.7 ft.to the South line of the property of Angel Grove Baptist
> Church as conveyed by Bessie Angel,a widow, et al to the Deacons of
> the Angel Grove Baptist Church on March 19, 1947 and recorded in the
> Probate Office of Calhoun County, Alabama in Book 847 at Page 197,
> thence S 88 degrees and 35 min. West 77.2 ft.to the Southwest corner
> of said church property, thence N 1 degree and 25 min.West 444.6 ft.
> to point of beginning. Containing 2.01 acres lying south of Ala. High-
> way No. 204 in the SE¼ of the NE¼ of Section 1, Township 14 South,
> Range 7 East and SW¼ of the NW¼ of Section 6, Township 14 South,
> Range 8 East.
> ALSO:
> 0.06 acres in the SW¼ of the NW¼ of Section 6, Township 14 South,
> Range 8 East described as beginning at a point on the South line
> of Ala Highway No. 204, said point being South 18 degrees and 04 min.
> East 1929 ft.from the Northwest corner of Section 6, thence South
> 70 degrees and 50 min.West 55.7 ft. to the East line of the property
> of Angel Grove Baptist Church, thence North 1 degree and 25 min.West
> along the East line of said Church 93.2 ft. to the South line of
> (con't. next page)

appurtenances thereunto belonging, or in anywise appertaining.

TO HAVE AND TO HOLD the said tract or parcel of land unto the

said   ANGEL GROVE BAPTIST CHURCH

their   heirs and assigns, in fee simple forever; and for the consideration aforesaid, we do for ourselves , for our heirs, executors
and administrators, successors and assigns, covenant to and with the
said   ANGEL GROVE BAPTIST CHURCH

that we a re lawfully seized and possessed in fee simple of said tract
or parcel of land; that we ha ve a good and lawful right to sell and
convey the same as aforesaid; that the same is free of all encumbrances,
except as herein stated; and that we will forever warrant and defend
the title thereto against the lawful claims of all persons whomsoever.

IN WITNESS WHEREOF, we have hereunto set our hands and seals
this the 31st day of DECEMBER, 1970.

_____ (SEAL)

_____ (SEAL)

Mrs. E.J. (Bessie) Angel

Mr. & Mrs. G.W. Angel

13

STATE OF ALABAMA,} This Indenture, Made and entered into this the 15th day of
CALHOUN COUNTY.}
May 1915, by and between Dave Cowden and wife, Kate Cowden
parties of the first part and
Angel Grove Baptist Church. parties of the second part.
WITNESSETH, That the parties of the first part, for and in consideration of the sum of
($5⁰⁰) Five and no/100 DOLLARS,

to them in hand paid, the receipt whereof is hereby acknowledged, hath granted, bargained and sold, and doth by these presents grant, bargain and sell, unto the said party of the second part, and unto his successors he and assigns, the following described real estate,

A certain parcel of land for church and cemetery purposes, situated in the S.E. ¼ of S.W. ¼ of Sec 36, T. 3, R. 7, but more particularly described as follows; Beginning on the Township line 231 feet west of half-Section corner, thence North 231 feet to the Gadsden Public road, thence west along said road 313½ feet thence south 297 feet to the Township line thence east on Township line 313½ feet to the point of beginning, Containing one and 90/100 acres. This deed is good as long as it is used for church or cemetery purposes.

situated in Calhoun County, Alabama, with all the tenements, and appurtenances thereunto belonging or in anywise appertain of

TO HAVE AND TO HOLD to the said party of the second part.

And we do covenant with the said Angel Baptist Church and their successors their successors and assigns that we are lawfully seized in fee of the aforegranted premises, that they are free from all incumbrances; that we have good right to sell and convey the same to said Angel Grove Baptist Church their successors heirs and assigns, and that we will warrant and defend the same unto said Angel Baptist Church their successors heirs and assigns forever, against the lawful claims and demands of all persons.

IN TESTIMONY WHEREOF, we have hereunto set our hands and seal s, this the 15th day of May, 1915.

Signed, Sealed and Delivered in the Presence of

J. F. Green

Dave Cowden. (L. S.)
Kate Cowden (L. S.)
(L. S.)
(L. S.)

THE STATE OF ALABAMA,} I, J. F. Green, a Notary Public
Calhoun County.} in and for said County, hereby certify that Dave Cowden and wife,
Kate Cowden, whose name s are signed to the foregoing conveyance, and who are known to me, acknowledged before me on this day that being informed of the contents of the conveyance, they executed the same voluntarily on the day the same bears date.
Given under my hand and seal, on the 15th day of May A. D. 1915.

J. F. Green
Notary Public

THE STATE OF ALABAMA,} I,
Calhoun County.} in and for said State and County, do hereby certify that on the day of
the within named
day of

In May of 1915 the nearby Seven Springs Cemetery was deeded to Angel Grove Church by Dave and Kate Cowden. The members of local churches organized the annual cleaning and decoration of the graves by hosting a "dinner on the grounds" and memorial service on the Saturday before the fourth Sunday in May.

Seven Springs Cemetery which was deeded to Angel Grove Church May 15, 1915 by Dave & Kate Cowden. Decorations are held on the 4th Saturday of May

THIS INDENTURE made and entered into on this the

_____ day of March, 1947, by and between:

        Mrs. Bessie Angel, a widow
        Louise Angel, an unmarried woman
        George William Angel and wife, Doris Angel,
        Janet Angel, an unmarried woman
        Geraldine Angel Nunnally and husband,
          L. C. Nunnally,
        Joyce Angel Lee and husband, James William Lee,
        Bernice Angel, an unmarried woman
        Eleanor Angel, an unmarried woman
  and Yvonne Angel, an unmarried woman.

parties of the first part, and

        J. M. Prickett
        I. A. Clark
        J. W. McDuffie
        F. T. Angel
        Clyde Brittain
  and W. H. Angel, as Deacons of Angel Grove Baptist

Church and their successors as such Deacons, parties of the secon

part:

    WITNESSETH:

    That, Whereas, the property herein conveyed belonged

to E. J. Angel at the time of his death in December, 1944;

    AND, WHEREAS, the parties of the first part constitute

all the heirs at law of said E. J. Angel, deceased;

    NOW, THEREFORE, in consideration of the sum of One

Dollar ($1.00) and other valuable considerations to the parties

of the first part in hand paid by the parties of the second part,

the receipt whereof is hereby acknowledged, the parties of the

first part have granted, bargained and sold, and do by these

presents grant, bargain, sell and convey unto the parties of

the second part, the following described real property, to-wit:

    Beginning at a point on the west boundary line of
    Section 6, Township 14 South, Range 8 East, which
    point is the SW corner of the church lot deeded
    By R. J. Angel and wife, Nannie E. Angel, to
    J. W. Propst and W. P. Turk, Deacons of Angel Grove
    Baptist Church and their successors in office, on

January 3, 1890, which deed is recorded in Volume 5, Page 202 in the Probate Office of Calhoun County, Alabama; thence in a general easterly direction along the south line of said church lot 270 feet to the southeast corner thereof; thence in a southerly direction 205 feet; thence west to the west boundary line of said Section 180 feet; thence north along said Section line 225 feet to the point of beginning; containing one and one-half acres, more or less, and being in the northwest quarter of said Section 6, Township 14 South, Range 8 East in Calhoun County, Alabama.

TO HAVE AND TO HOLD, together with all and singular the rights, tenements, hereditaments, and appurtenances thereunto belonging or in anywise appertaining, unto the parties of the second part, their successors and assigns, in fee simple.

And the parties of the first part do hereby covenant with the parties of the second part that they are lawfully seized in fee of the said premises, that they have a good right to sell and convey the same; that said premises are free from incumbrance; and that they warrant, and will forever defend the title to said premises against the lawful claims and demands of all persons whomsoever.

IN WITNESS WHEREOF, the parties of the first part have hereto set their hand and seals, on this, the day and year herein first above written.

_____ (L.S.)   _____ (L.S.)

Louise Angel _____ (L.S.)   Jasper Angel Lee ____ (L.S.)

George William Angel (L.S.)   _____ William ____ (L.S.)
Doris Angel

_____ (L.S.)   _____ Angel ____ (L.S.)

Janet Angel _____ (L.S.)   Eleanor Angel ____ (L.S.)

Geraldine Angel Nunnally (L.S.)   Yvonne Angel ____ (L.S.)

August 7, 1920 -- "The following brothers were elected deacons: Bro. H.E. Wynn, Bro. Willie Lanford, Bro. Lee Gardner, Bro. S.T. Moore. The church decided to run meeting one sermon a day and one at night."

February 7, 1921 -- A brother was "brought up in conference." Pastor Stephens made a statement that the brother had told him that he "was going to do better which was accepted. Bro. H.E. Wynn was elected chairman of the building committee."

July 30, 1921 -- "Brother Stephens resigned as pastor, and the church elected Brother G.S. Morris as pastor for the ensuing year." (Pastors served one-year terms.)

October 22, 1921 -- "Brother Wynn asked the church what they were going to do about the pledge money. They decided to let the old manager to get it up."

November 26, 1921 -- "The church decided to get up some minute money" to purchase copies of the associational minutes.

January 22, 1922 -- "A move was made to put the Alabama Baptist newspaper in the budget of the church. A committee of three was to work the plan up. Brother A.L. Weaver was chairman. Miss Annis Owens and Miss Trannie Couch was to help on the committee."

April 22, 1922 -- The church "voted to build the bookcase back where it was. The bill of the expenses of painting the church" totaled $57.73. "A committee of three brethren was to fix the table. A committee of three girls - Miss Annis Owens, Miss Arrie Owens, and Miss Trannie Couch - was to get up money for Brother Morris to help pay his fare to Jacksonville, Florida. Brother H.E. Wynn and W. B. Lanford were appointed to get up what money they could on the pledges."

June 24, 1922 -- "It was suggested that the well be cleaned out and cemented up around the top. Brother Albert Buchannan agreed to clean out the well. The church agreed to do the concrete work."

August 27, 1922 -- "Reverend G.S. Morris was unanimously re-elected pastor" for the coming year. "The church extended an arm to Cedar Springs schoolhouse to receive members."

September 23, 1922 -- "There was a committee appointed to see each member and get them to say what they will give each month to the support of pastor and church. The clerk and A.L. Weaver were the committee. Brother Tom Angel is to collect the money each month."

November 25, 1922 -- "Brothers J.P. McKowen, Lee Andrews, and W. B. Lanford were appointed to buy the new stove."

May 26, 1923 -- "By a motion and second a committee consisting of Sisters Trannie Couch, Alice Moore, Annie Wynn, and Brother Will Angel were appointed to raise money and get new lights for the church before the protracting meeting in July."

June 23, 1923 -- "Miss Annis Owens was added to the committee that was to get up money to buy the new lights. The committee asked the church what kind of lights they wanted to buy. The kind West Point is using was suggested."

July 28, 1923 -- "Reverend G.S. Mooris was nominated and was unanimously re-elected."

September 22, 1923 -- "By request of Brother Morris, a motion carried for him to try to get up a preacher's school at our church in the near future."

October 27, 1923 -- "A communication in regard to the preacher's school was read by our pastor, and a committee consisting of Sisters Nannie Angel, Zula Mae Burgess, and Ethel Angel and Brother J.P. McKowen to secure lodging for the visiting ministers that would be in attendance."

October 28, 1923 -- "The committee having made an unfavorable report as to securing lodging for the visiting ministers, it was voted not to have the preacher's school."

March 22, 1924 -- A written acknowledgment was received from a brother "asking the church to forgive him for some unchristian conduct that he had been participating in which was accepted...A motion carried to appoint a committee to see another brother "about some unchristian conduct reports on him."

June 22, 1924 -- The brother "not being present to make a statement in his own behalf in regards to the reports on him, by a vote of the church charges were preferred and fellowship withdrawn from him for contempt of the church."

August 6, 1924 -- (Angel Grove and Post Oak Church shared a circuit pastor.) "A vote was taken to consolidate Angel Grove Church and Post Oak Springs Church. Vote carried to retain Angel Grove at the present site and enlarge the building. Motion carried for same committee, T.R. Bryant, Will Angel, W. B. Lanford, J.P. McKowen, and I.A. Clark," to plan the building...Brother Morris was elected pastor for the coming year.

August 23, 1924 -- "D.D. Weaver, chairman of a committee from Post Oak Springs Church stated that he was appointed to confer with this church as to the two churches building a pastor's home at Cedar Springs. The proposition was left to a vote of this church and lost."

September 27, 1924 -- "Brother E. J. Clark extended an invitation to the eldership of this church to Friendship Church on the first Sunday in October to assist in the ordination of some deacons for that church."

May 24, 1925 -- "The committee appointed to have the church enlarged reported that they could get the work done for $95.00 if the church would furnish materials. The committee of young ladies appointed by the building committee to raise funds reported having $138.00 promised. The committee was given more time and authorized to have work done. By motion, a vote was taken to move the church down near the graveyard. The vote resulted in retaining the church at the present site."

August 1, 1925 -- "Re-elected Brother Morris as pastor for the next pastoral year...Brothers W.H. and F.T. Angel were elected deacons of this church to be ordained at the regular meeting in August...The church voted unanimously to ask the association to meet with this church on the regular time in 1926."

August 22, 1925 -- "The ordination of the deacons was put off until the fifth Sunday in August, at which time Angel Grove and Post Oak Springs churches are to ordain for both churches jointly."

October 24, 1925 -- "A motion was carried to let the girls give a box supper for the purpose of raising money to paint the church."

October 25, 1925 -- "The deacons met and appointed a committee to raise money for covering the church and buying new benches."

January 23, 1926 -- "A motion was carried to get more coal. It was agreed to sell the chairs and buy new benches."

February 27, 1926 -- "A motion was carried to buy new song books."

July 31, 1926 -- Reverend G.S. Morris was re-elected as pastor for the coming year...A committee was appointed to secure places for visiting brethren who came to the association and wished to stay overnight. They were: Mrs. Ethel Angel, Miss Ola Owens, Miss Annie Wynn, and Mr. W.S. Bowling. The committee that got up the money to buy the rugs were released having bought them. Mr. Jim McKowen and Mr. W.O. Vineyard were appointed to fix up a place for the church stove."

August 21, 1926 -- "By a vote of the church, an arm was extended to the meeting to be held at Cedar Springs schoolhouse beginning August 29th."

September 5, 1926 -- "The treasurer made report that the church was about $35.00 short of what we paid last year for the pastor's salary." A brother "said he didn't think the church understood that there was any fixed salary. So on motion with a second, the members were asked to express their opinions as to how they understood it. By a rising vote, the church expressed an opinion as not understanding that there were any fixed salary. A motion carried to make up and pay Brother Morris the balance behind up to the amount paid the previous year. Also, the deacons were appointed to notify Brother Morris that the church would do the best they could the coming year, but did not promise any definite amount." (a hat was passed before the preaching services began, and the amount of the offering was the amount the preacher received for the week.)

September 26, 1926 -- "Brother Morris offered his resignation as pastor. The church voted unanimously not to accept it. Brother Morris again accepted the church...Brother Morris asked the church to lend him the song books for one of his other churches in the near future."

November 27, 1926 -- "A motion carried to call the roll of the church at the next regular meeting on Sunday and the members are to act as a committee to ask all to be present at that time."

December 26, 1926 -- "A motion carried to recover the old part of the church with galvanized metal roofing. T.R. Bryant, F.T. Angel, and A.L. Weaver were appointed as a committee to get the material and have the work done and present the bill to the church for payment."

February 26, 1927 -- "The committee on the covering of the church made report. They had the material ready so Thursday, March 3, was set to meet and do the work."

March 26, 1927 -- "A motion carried to invite the sister churches in the community to commune with our church at our regular meeting in May."

August 28, 1927 -- Reverend G.S. Morris was re-elected as pastor.

September 25, 1927 -- "Brother F.R. Mullino and Miss Vera Mullino were received as members of this church. Also, Brother Mullino was received as a deacon."

November 26, 1927 -- "A motion with a second carried to take a special collection at the eleven o'clock services on tomorrow for the Orphan's Home as a Christmas present to be sent to them after the third Sunday in December."

June 24, 1928 -- "Members agreed to meet Monday, June 25 to build concrete steps to each side door of the church."

July, 1928 -- 30 members joined during the protracting meeting.

August 25, 1928 -- "Brother Morris tendered his resignation as pastor asking Brother S.T. Moore to act as moderator while he retired from the house. The church went into the election of pastor, re-electing Brother Morris as pastor for the next year."

September 22, 1928 -- "Brother Morris tendered his resignation as pastor, which was accepted by the church."

September 23, 1928 -- "A committee consisting of F.T. Angel, T.R. Bryant, and A.L. Weaver were appointed as a pulpit committee to confer with the Post Oak deacons to see if they could get a preacher to recommend to the two churches."

November 25, 1928 -- "A committee consisting of officers and teachers of Sunday School was appointed to arrange a program for the Christmas Tree to be given December 24. A motion carried to hold Thanksgiving services here next Thursday." (The church celebrated with a Christmas Tree program each year.)

December 23, 1928 -- "A motion carried to go into the election of a pastor to serve the remainder of the pastoral year. Brother S.T. Moore acted as moderator protem while Reverend Lofton Abrams was nominated and elected."

March 24, 1929 -- "A committee consisting of the deacons and clerk was appointed to see about getting new lights for the church."

June 23, 1929 -- "The chairman of the light committee reported that the lights had been temporarily installed for the approval of the church."   August 3, 1929 -- "The church went into the election of a pastor...Brother Abrams was unanimously elected pastor for the next pastoral year."

August 24, 1929 -- "Motion made by Brother T.R. Bryant carried giving Reverend G.S. Mooris the authority to take or receive members into Angel Grove Church at his meeting to be held at Cedar Springs schoolhouse the first week of September. By request of brethren, the church loaned their benches for the meeting." (The meeting was held each fall.)

September 21, 1929 -- "A committee consisting of Mrs. Maggie Wynn, J.P. McKowen, and W.H. Angel was appointed to collect money and get a new organ for the church. Reverend E.J. Clark, with the deacons, was appointed as a committee to invite the other Baptist churches in the community to commune with us at our next regular meeting in October."

November 23, 1929 -- "Brother W.H. Angel, chairman of the committee to purchase an organ for the church made a report that there was not enough cash on hand to purchase the one selected and asked for an addition to the committee to assist in raising the funds. The following people were added to the committee: Miss Annis Owens, Mrs. Ethel Angel, and Miss Trannie Couch. Motion carried for the pastor to appoint a committee tomorrow to canvas the church and get pledges to the Cooperative Program. The following were appointed on the committee: Brothers T.R. Bryant, Marvin Nance, A.L. Weaver, Jim Johnson, and Roy Couch."

February 22, 1930 -- During the Sunday School report, it was suggested that "the weekly teachers' meeting be held in connection with the mid-week prayer meeting. The six-point record system was adopted for the Sunday School."

March 22, 1930 -- "Motion carried for treasurer's finance report to be included in the minutes each month. Amount collected on the pastor's salary to date is $100.50; amount for incidentals is $8.62; the Cooperative Program is $12.80."

June 21, 1930 -- "Brother Abrams tendered his resignation as pastor, to be in effect at the end of the pastoral year."

July 26, 1930 -- "It being the regular time for the election of pastor and clerk, the church went into the election by secret ballot. A motion with second carried for...three visiting brethren to act as tellers to count the votes. Motion to admit absentee votes and after discussion, adopted.   Motion carried for names to be signed to all ballots. Reverend G.S. Morris and Reverend L.L. Abrams were nominated for pastor. Brother Abrams received the majority of votes cast and was declared elected. On motion by Brother S.T. Moore, a rising vote was taken and the election was declared unanimous."

August 23, 1930 -- The church was asked "to extend an arm to a meeting to be held at Cedar Springs by Reverend G.S. Mooris beginning August 31st. Also, asked to borrow some of the church benches, which was granted."

September 27, 1930 -- "A motion carried to get Reverend L.A. Beasley to teach a three day Bible School at this church on 28, 29, and 30th of November. The pastor's salary for the last pastoral year ending September the 14th, 1930 was $171.55."

October 25, 1930 -- A brother "made a statement that he and one of the other brethren of the church had had a difficulty and that he was sorry of it and was willing to make friends with the brother at any time. He stated he believed he had made it right with his Lord and asked forgiveness of the church which was granted by a vote of the church."

November 22, 1930 -- "By request of the entertainment committee appointed yesterday for the Bible Institute, a vote was taken and went unanimous to serve lunch at the church on Thanksgiving Day." (This Thanksgiving dinner was an annual event for several years.)

June 27, 1931 -- "After some discussion, it was voted to have a Sunday School training class in our Sunday School..."

July 25, 1931 -- A brother "asked the church to extend an arm to Brother G.S. Morris and Mr. Daniel's meeting at Cedar Spring...which after some discussion was granted, but with some opposition."

September 13, 1931 -- "Motion and second that we go into the election of pastor for the ensuing year carried. Motion and second to elect by acclamation carried. Brother Henry Harris was nominated and carried unanimously."

November 15, 1931 -- Brother Walt Vineyard and his family joined the church. "Brother Vineyard was received as an ordained deacon." A committee was formed to "collect supplies for the Orphan's Home...Motion and second that Cedar Springs Sunday School be allowed to retain five dollars of the Cotton Patch Money to finish paying for song books carried. (Each farmer set aside a portion of his cotton patch for the church.)

December 19, 1931 -- "The clerk stated that he had turned over to the treasurer of Cedar Springs some Cotton Patch Money in the amount of $12.78."

February 20, 1932 -- "The Orphan's Home Committee reported the value of the stuff sent to the home at $30.00."

May 14, 1932 -- "Motion and second that we buy some lights for the church and pay for them out of the church treasury carried." A Baptist Young People's Union (BYPU) was established.

July 16, 1932 -- "The committee to purchase lights reported that they had received the lights and put them up at a cost of $13.98...It was agreed that we meet on Wednesday before the fifth Sunday and clean the church grounds and scrub the floors."

August 20, 1932 -- "Motion and second that we go into the election of pastor for the ensuing year carried...and unanimously elected Brother W.H. Harris." A motion and second carried to "extend an arm to the meeting of Brothers G.S. Morris and W.H. Harris at Cedar Springs schoolhouse...for the acceptation of members in this church in any way that the gospel authorizes."

September 17, 1932 -- "This church invited Mt. Gilead, Pleasant Valley, and West Point to commune with us on the 4th Sunday in October."

October 22, 1932 -- "The pastor presented to the church a plan given by the Octagon Soap Products in which a cash value will be given to the Baptist Orphan's Home. That being adopted, a committee was appointed of Mrs. W.H. Harris, Mrs. J.P. McKowen, and Miss Annis Owens to collect the coupons."

November 27, 1932 -- "There was a committee appointed by the Sunday School to take up offering for the Orphan's Home at Troy, Alabama...That committee visited all the members of the church and received about $21.71 worth of food stuff."

February 25, 1933 -- "The church adopted a plan to raise some money for missions. Each one will pledge so many pounds of cotton. This was adopted."

April 22, 1933 -- "Motion and second that Brothers E.J. Clark and Tom Angel give the wood that they cut at the graveyard to someone for firewood."

August 6, 1933 -- "Reverend W.H. Harris was elected pastor."

September 10, 1933 -- "As no money was appropriated from the treasury for associational minutes, it was decided to let all who wanted minutes pay 15 cents to one of the delegates to be turned in at the association. Ninety cents was turned in, the clerk keeping the list of those paying."

September 23, 1933 -- "The question of the cotton pledges for the mission and incidental expenses of the church was brought up. It was suggested that the cotton be brought to the gin by September 26."

November 26, 1933 -- "By motion and second, the treasurer was authorized to sell the cotton pledged for the missions and incidental expenses of the church and take charge of the funds." (The treasurer at this time owned the cotton gin.)

December 23, 1933 -- "Treasurer reported $36.02 turned in on cotton pledges to date. By move and second, the treasurer was authorized to pay the housekeeper monthly out of the treasury."

July 21, 1934 -- Charges were preferred against a brother 'for departing from the faith and, by vote of the church, fellowship withdrawn."

August 5, 1934 -- "after preaching by Brother G.S. Morris, Brother Harris retired from the house, and Brother Morris was elected moderator protem while the election of pastor and clerk for the ensuing year. The regular order of election was waived and Reverend W.H. Harris was unanimously re-elected by nomination and acclamation. The deacons were appointed as a committee to notify him."

August 25, 1934 -- "Action on motion to elevate church building was postponed temporarily...Motion carried to give wood contained in a dead tree to someone to cut it."

August 26, 1934 -- "By move and second, there was an appropriation of $10 to be paid to the State Baptist Executive Board for the Cooperative Program...By move and second the church extended an arm to receive members in a revival to be held at Cedar Springs the first week in September."

November 25, 1934 -- "The deacons reported on the finance plan for the church, and by move and second, the committee was released with the suggestion that the church pursue the same financial plan used in the past. Contributions were urged for the Orphan's Home produce car." (Food goods were shipped to the Home.)

December 23, 1934 -- "Committee on Orphan's Home produce car reported approximately $20.00 for contributions."

January 27, 1935 -- "The church voted to elect a collector to assist the treasurer in collecting the pastor's salary." (The treasurer had had to see each member personally for donations for the pastor's salary.)

June 23, 1935 -- "The matter of cleaning church grounds and repairing the table was brought before the church. Friday morning, June 28 was set as a date for meeting and attending to same."

August 3, 1934 -- "Move and second to go into election of pastor...Reverend Harris received a majority and his election was made unanimous...A flower service was held Saturday evening in honor and appreciation of the services of Reverend and Mrs. Harris. A brief talk was made by Reverend E.J. Clark. Reverend and Mrs. Harris responded with short talks."

August 24, 1935 -- "By request of the young people, Brother J.P. McKowen asked that they be allowed to purchase a piano for the church. A vote was taken and the request was unanimously in favor of same."

August 25, 1935 -- "A committee consisting of T.R. Bryant, Samuel Wilson, R.W. Couch, Robert Clark, Herbert Smith, and Miss Annis Owens was appointed to raise funds and purchase a piano."

September 21, 1935 -- "The church voted to take part in a Mock Trial (a play) to be presented at Cedar Springs on October 25 by Judge R.B. Carr, S.L. Johnson, and others of Anniston."

January 25, 1936 -- "The committee appointed to raise money and purchase a piano, made a report that they had purchased one and paid for same...A committee consisting of Brothers H.E. Wynn, E.J. Angel, and Samuel Wilson were appointed to purchase a Delco Light Plant for the church."

March 22, 1936 -- "The young people asked the church to cooperate with them in putting on a play to raise funds to do some repairs to the church. They were bid Godspeed by the pastor in behalf of the church."

April 25, 1936 -- "The chairman of the committee to have the heater flue built made a report that owing to the treasury funds being low and warm weather on hand; they had not had the work done. The report was accepted. Brother H.E. Wynn reported that the light plant was installed."

August 1, 1936 -- "Motion and second carried to dispense with the regular rules and elect by nomination and acclamation. Brother Harris's name, being the only one placed in nomination, was unanimously elected as pastor for the next pastoral year."

August 21, 1937 -- "A motion and second was carried that funds be raised to repaint our church. The following were appointed as a committee: W.H. Angel, chairman; Mrs. Oscar Couch; Mrs. Samuel Wilson; and Mrs. Hubert Boozer...Brother Harris was nominated and elected as pastor without an opposition. Brother E.J. Clark was elected as assistant pastor and is to receive one-third of the pastor's salary."

September 26, 1937 -- "The following new business was attended to: 1. voted to connect church to Alabama Power Company for lighting system and to take a collection for same; 2. voted to elect deacons to be ordained in October. The following were selected: Clyde Brittain, Samuel Wilson, and Robert Clark."

October 26, 1937 -- "Motion and second to give Brother Will Angel the old organ to pay for same." (He had paid for the organ when the church was unable to do so.)

December 26, 1937 -- The church voted to discharge two sisters "for departing from our faith."

August 27, 1938 -- "A request was made that the Rules of Decorum be read..." (The Rules of Decorum had been read before all business meetings in the earlier days.)

October, 1938 -- "There was a move and second that the church go into the election of pastor. The motion was carried that the election be held by acclamation. Reverend Leslie Hall was nominated and elected as pastor without an opposition."

July 23, 1939 -- "There was a motion and second carried that the church go into the election of officers of the church. The motion was carried that we elect by acclamation. Reverend Leslie Hall was nominated and elected as pastor without an opposition..."

August 27, 1939 -- A committee was appointed "to collect money for a radio program to be conducted by Reverend Ira Harris and dedicated to Angel Grove Baptist Church."

September, 1939 -- "The Angel Grove Missionary Baptist Church licensed Brother Harold Smith to preach the gospel."

December, 1939 -- "The Angel Grove Baptist Church licensed Brother Lester Clark to preach the gospel."

April, 1940 -- "A letter from Gold Ridge Baptist Church asking this church to help them with their new building was read. Then, a collection of $3.15 was taken up to be sent to the clerk of their church."

July, 1940 -- "There was a motion and second carried that the church go into the election of officers for the church...Reverend Leslie Hall was nominated and elected as pastor without an opposition."

December, 1940 -- "There was a move and second that pledges be accepted for pastor's salary...Deacons serve as a committee to contact each member and see how much each can pledge."

February, 1941 -- "Vote and second to send Sunday School offering to Temperance Committee. Vote was held and carried to make plans to build a new church. Move and second that Reverend Leslie Hall appoint a committee to see about the pledges to be made to raise sufficient funds to build a church. The following were appointed on the committee: Mose Prickett, Will Angel, Edd Moore, and Mrs. Annie Johnson."

March, 1941 -- "After a discussion of discontinuing the Saturday service, there was a move and second that the Saturday service be discontinued and another Sunday service be added the third Sunday to be continued throughout the present year. We also voted to have a singing the fifth Sunday in June."

July, 1941 -- "There was a move and second that the pastor be elected by nomination and acclamation. Brother Leslie Hall and Brother H.E. Boozer being nominated, there was a move and second that nominations be closed. Brother Emmett Boozer received a majority of votes and was declared elected. On a motion another vote was taken and the election was declared unanimous."

September, 1941 -- The Sunday School classes were given authority to buy a pulpit Bible. (The offering taken during Sunday School classes was kept separately from the offering taken during the preaching services.

October, 1941 -- "After discussion...a decision was made to turn all the money in to Brother J.M. Prickett" when it was collected for the new church building.

November, 1941 -- "A report was made by Brother J.M. Prickett, chairman of the Building Committee, requesting everyone to turn their money in immediately to members of the committee. There was a unanimous vote for a Christmas Tree, plans to be made later."

January, 1942 -- "Brother J.M. Prickett reported on the building committee and asked that all pledges be turned in as soon as possible."

March 22, 1942 -- "Suggestions were made to elect three new deacons. After discussion, Brothers Jack McDuffie, Robert Johnson, and Mose Prickett were nominated and elected as candidates for deacons."

June 28, 1942 -- "Brother Prickett made a request urging all members to pay their pledges toward the building of the new church building. After preaching, Communion services were held."

August 2, 1942 -- "Brother Emmett Boozer, the present pastor was duly nominated and duly elected without opposition."

September 27, 1942 -- "This day was set aside by our church to honor and entertain a number of men in the armed forces from Fort McClellan, Alabama. There being sixty-five in number...Services were conducted under the leadership of Chaplain F.B. Samson...Dinner was spread and the jubilee invited to eat. After the lunch hour, several songs were sung and special numbers were rendered by men from Fort McClellan."

December 27, 1942 -- "Brother Prickett made a report of $482.74 having been collected toward the building of a new church and urged everyone to pay their pledges. Move was made and duly seconded that the church take a vote as to the location of the new church. The location on the hill behind the present building was decided upon and the church by a unanimous vote adopted that location."

April 25, 1943 -- "Brother J.M. Prickett made an appeal urging all members to pay their pledges toward the building of the new church now."

June 27, 1943 -- "At the noon hour, lunch was spread on the church grounds and a group of soldiers from Fort McClellan were invited as special guests. After which they rendered a program conducted by Chaplain Samson who presented the church Honor Roll and flag to the pastor, Brother Boozer, in honor and memory of our boys in the armed forces of our country."

August 1, 1943 -- "Motion was made and seconded to elect by acclamation Brother Emmett Boozer. Brother Boozer was nominated and unanimously elected without opposition." September 26, 1943 -- "Brother J.M. Prickett made report on the new church program, stating to date $657.74 had been paid."

April 30, 1944 -- "Today was set aside by the church to entertain a group of soldiers and their chaplain from Fort McClellan...An inspiring message was delivered by Chaplain Samson after which, dinner was served...During the afternoon services, singing and special music was enjoyed by the church and a number of visitors."

July 29, 1944 -- Reverend Emmett Boozer was re-elected as pastor "unanimously without opposition and not one dissenting vote being cast."

November 26, 1944 -- "The church voted to have the Christmas Tree on December 23 this year (instead of Christmas Eve night since that would be Sunday night). Motion was made and carried to appoint a standing committee to take care of having flowers or wreaths made to give our members when death comes to their families. Committee appointed: Sisters Ethel Angel and Annis Owens."

July 29, 1945 -- "Brother Emmett Boozer was elected unanimously without opposition as pastor."

November 25, 1945 -- "Brother Prickett made a report on the money collected toward building the new church. The amount being $755.74 to date. Plans are being discussed and agreed upon. A meeting of the deacons was called for November 29th at Brother Will Angel's house with every member being invited. The purpose of this meeting being to further plan the new church building." June 23, 1946 -- "Brothers Roy Couch, J.M. Prickett, and J.D. Pritchett were appointed on a committee to raise funds and purchase new song books."

August 3, 1946 -- "The following were appointed to serve on a committee to secure a preacher for the next meeting day, and investigate who can serve as pastor, and who the church might want: Brothers Joe Wilson, Tom Angel, and Robert Johnson...Motion was made and carried to give the housekeeper $2.00 per month."

August 25, 1946 -- "The church went into the election of pastor for the ensuing year. Brother Henry Harris was nominated and elected unanimously without opposition."

December 22, 1946 -- A motion made and carried that a gift box be placed at the Christmas Tree and be a part of the program. The proceeds be a gift to Christ and used in the building of our new church building."

January 26, 1947 -- "Report was made regarding proceeds from the Christmas Tree. The amount received in cash and pledges amounting to $64.80 making a grand total of $1457.54. A committee was appointed by Brother Harris to draw up plans for the new church building and present to the church for approval and go forward with the construction work. The committee is as follows: W.H. Angel, R.W. Couch, I.A. Clark, J.R. Angel, Bud Burgess, J.H. Wilson, and Clyde Brittain."

February 23, 1947 -- "Brother W.H. Angel reported the deeds to the new church grounds were being prepared and would be completed in a short time. The plans of the new building were presented by Brother Harris. Upon a motion and second, the plans were adopted and the building committee empowered to purchase material and proceed with the construction of the new building as soon as deeds are completed. Brother Prickett reported the women had raised $107.50 from hens sold...bringing the balance to $1666.04 to date." (The women boiled hens in a pot over an open fire and sold them in Jacksonville.)

February 23, 1947 -- "The church voted to sponsor Brother Harris' radio program once a month, taking a collection each fourth Sunday night - the proceeds to be for that purpose.

March, 1947 -- "Brother Angel reported the deeds to the new church grounds were completed. Motion made and carried empowering the building committee to buy materials. A report was made that a total of $1744.74 had been collected to date on the new church building."

April 27, 1947 -- "Brother Prickett reported cash on hand to date was $994.15 after $1028.39 had been paid out...The women were reported to have raised $95.00 since the last meeting."

August 3, 1947 -- "The church voted the building committee the authority to sell the surplus material in the old church building not needed in the construction of the new building." (Some of the materials from the old church were used in the construction of the new building.)

August 24, 1947 - The church met with West Point for regular worship services. Reverend Henry Harris was elected without opposition. "A public subscription was held for the new church building and $550.00 was raised." (The church met at West Point Church because the old church had been torn down and the new building was not completed.)

October 26, 1947 -- "A public subscription was held at this time and a total of $854.00 was raised and pledged toward the completion of the building. (Members made their pledges orally before the congregation.)

November 23, 1947 -- "The following were appointed on a committee to collect clothing to be sent to Europe: Mrs. John Owens, Frances Wilson, and Mrs. Harold Smith." (The clothes were needed, of course, because of World War II.)

February 22, 1948 -- "Brother Harris read a receipt from the State Executive Board showing that the church had contributed $100.00 to the Cooperative Program. Also read was a statement from the Southern Baptist Relief Center saying that they had received 87 pounds of clothing from the church to be sent to the needy people in war-torn areas."

March 28, 1948 -- "A report was made that $100.00 had been paid on the new benches, and that they were complete, the remainder to be paid when they were delivered. The women were asked to stain the benches. Motion was made and seconded to have the building completed and to have the dedication the fourth Sunday in April, to be an all day affair with lunch served." April 25, 1948 -- "Today before preaching by our pastor, Brother Harris, it was decided not to have a formal conference due to the services of the day. No business was transacted. This being the day for the dedication of our new church, completed free of debt. After the morning services by our pastor, lunch was spread on the grounds. In the afternoon Brother Morris had charge of the devotional, then all former pastors present were asked to make talks. The following were present: Brother G.S. Morris, Brother E.J. Clark, and Brother Leslie Hall. Reverend B.B. Burkes of Southside delivered the dedication sermon. An individual communion set was presented to the church as a gift from the Mt. Gilead Baptist Church."

May 23, 1948 -- "Brother Prickett made a final report on the building fund. To date $5029.10 had been collected and $5029.10 had been paid out, leaving a balance of $51.26 which Brother Prickett was to keep until asked for by the church."

August 22, 1948 -- "The following church officers were elected to serve this year: Brother Henry Harris, pastor...Motion and second was made that a loud speaker be acquired for the singing convention and the church would pay for it." (Angel Grove hosted this convention each fall for almost 40 years.)

September 26, 1948 -- "Our invitation was accepted for the association to convene with us the first day next year, this day being changed to Tuesday following the second Sunday in September." The church voted to "have services two Sundays a month, the second and the fourth. The committee to see about the heating system was asked to make a report. It was reported that we could secure Butane gas, including a tank and four heaters for

$350.00...It was accepted, and it was decided that $100 be taken out of the Sunday School money, and the remaining of the building fund money be paid on this, and the committee collect the balance."

October 14, 1948 -- "Brother Prickett presented a bill to the church of $382.00, total expenses for the heating system. $193.75 was needed to finish paying the bill. Pledges were made from the congregation to pay the balance."

December 12, 1948 -- "All bills had been paid with $10.00 left in the treasury."

January 23, 1949 -- A committee of Mr. Roy Couch, Mrs. Annie Johnson, Mrs. Herbert Smith, and Mrs. Winston Wilson were appointed to see about getting shrubbery for the church grounds."

March 27, 1949 -- "Mr. Roy Couch, chairman of the shrubbery committee reported that Mr. Longshore had been contacted and that he would put out shrubbery for $50.00...Mr. Mose Prickett reported that 50 gallons of gas had been put in the tank, and paid for out of heating system money...which left him a balance of $3.00 which was turned over to the church treasury.."

May 22, 1949 -- "The song book committee reported $52.00 had been raised to pay on the books."

July 24, 1949 -- "Reverend Henry Harris was nominated and elected without opposition as pastor."

August 14, 1949 -- "A committee consisting of Tom Angel, Jack McDuffie, Harold Smith, Robert Johnson, and Bud Burgess was appointed and given authority to spend money in the treasury to buy meat for the association."

September 25, 1949 -- "A motion was made that we send a card of thanks to West Point and Post Oak for their offering helping to feed the people at our association. A report was made that we owed $71.74 balance on the meat and supplies bought for the associational dinner. Motion and second was made that we pay the balance out of the Sunday School money with anyone helping that wanted to."

November 27, 1949 -- "The treasurer reported that $59.00 had been collected on the Howard College fund."

September 24, 1950 -- "A motion and second was made that we elect a pastor for another year. Reverend Fred Curvin and Wilfred Pritchard were nominated. Reverend Curvin received the majority of the votes. Then the church voted unanimously for Reverend Curvin."

March 25, 1951 -- "After a short discussion on the new communion table for our church, a motion and second was made that the committee decide on the kind to get and go ahead and buy it."

June 24, 1951 -- "The following were recommended by the board of deacons to be ordained as new deacons for the church: Brothers Doyle Pritchett, Harold Littlejohn, Curtis Johnson, and Clytus Angel. After a motion and second, the church voted to accept them into deaconship...Mrs. Tom Angel and Mrs. Doyle Pritchett were released as a committee for getting a new table for the church. A motion and second was made that we release the old piano and $100.00 from the church treasury on the purchase of a new piano. Mrs. Doyle Pritchett, Mrs. Johnnie Brittain, Mrs. Robert Johnson, Tom Angel, and Roy Couch were appointed as a committee to buy the piano."

July 22, 1951 -- "Reverend Fred Curvin was elected pastor without opposition...The church gave the deacons the authority to sign the deeds for the right of way for the new highway." (Highway 204 was under construction.)

January 27, 1952 -- "By request of the pastor, 10% of the morning offering will be put in the church treasury."

July 27, 1952 -- "Reverend Fred Curvin was elected pastor without opposition...The church voted to go on full time." (The church began having services each Sunday.)

September 14, 1952 -- "Brother Mose Prickett made a report on the condition of the church floor. After a discussion, a committee was appointed to make plans on installing the floor and the type to be used. Those on the committee were: R.M. Johnson, chairman; J.M. Prickett, W.H. Angel, and Harold Littlejohn."

September 28, 1952 -- "R.M. Johnson, chairman of the floor committee, made a report that the committee had decided to pour a concrete floor. A special offering was taken to finance this job."

November 23, 1952 -- "It was agreed that we pay our pastor the first $25.00 of our Sunday morning's offering, the balance to go in the general treasury."

January 25, 1953 -- "For the past nine weeks, the church has taken in $517.94. Pastor's salary was $225.00; expenses $59.62, leaving a balance of $233.32 in the church treasury. The Sunday School has $231.98 on hand."

February 22, 1953 -- "The pastor was given the authority to appoint a president for the Vacation Bible School."

April 26, 1953 -- "A motion was made and seconded that the moderator appoint a committee to draw plans on finishing the front of our church. Those appointed were Will Angel, Curtis Johnson, I.A. Clark, and Bill McDuffie. The committee appointed to draw up plans for Sunday School rooms were as follows: J.M. Prickett, Harold Littlejohn, Doyle Pritchett, and Clytus Angel. The finance committee were: Robert Johnson, Tom Angel, Joe Johnson, and Lawrence Burgess."

July 26, 1953 -- "A motion and second was made that we blacktop as much of the ground as needed in front of the church with the church paying half of the expenses and the Sunday School paying the other half. Brothers Mose Prickett, Tom Angel, and Lawrence Burgess were appointed as a committee to see to this matter. The church agreed to pay Reverend Curvin a bonus of $125.00 on Sunday, August 2. Reverend Curvin offered his resignation as pastor of the church."

September 16, 1953 -- "Reverend George Vines was recommended and elected by the church to serve for coming year...The church voted to omit the intermission between Sunday School and preaching."

October 25, 1953 -- "The church voted to give the pastor the morning offering after all expenses were paid. The Training Union was given the authority to paint the church on the inside."

November 22, 1953 -- "By a vote of the church, it was decided to paint the church two shades of green...A move and second was made that we adopt the use of visitor's cards...Mrs. Tom Angel, Mrs. Doyle Pritchett, and Mrs. Annie McDuffie were appointed to buy new curtains and a pulpit stand."

January 24, 1954 -- "Mrs. Tom Angel reported that the curtains were finished and up, and the pulpit wasn't complete. The church voted to give the pastor $35.00 each Sunday if the offering is that much after expenses are paid, and the rest to go into the building fund."

April 25, 1954 -- "A motion and second was made that the amount of the morning offering be put on the bottom of the Sunday School report board after services."

June 27, 1954 -- "After a discussion on whether to remain full time or go half time, the church voted to remain full time. The church accepted Reverend Vines' resignation, effective the second Sunday in July."

August 22, 1954 -- "Reverend Albert Bowman was nominated and elected without opposition to serve as pastor for the coming year. The church voted to have preaching four Sundays a month with each fifth Sunday being open."

October 24, 1954 -- "A motion was approved for the church to pay for the Alabama Baptist paper to be sent to all the church families who requested it. The paper has been sent into twelve homes. Motion was made and approved to have conference every fourth Sunday just after Sunday School."

December 26, 1954 -- "A report was given that a total of $158.00 was given for storm relief." (A tornado had ripped through the community.)

February 27, 1955 -- "Minutes of the last conference were read. They were amended to eliminate every committee and motion or anything the church had passed upon, so as to give the pastor a clean slate prior to the appointment of the present pastor."

March 27, 1955 -- "Motion was made and passed for the pastor to appoint a planning committee. J.L. Johnson, Will S. Prickett, I.A. Clark, Harold Littlejohn, and Jasper Nolan were appointed. Clytus Angel was nominated and elected to be in charge of the building of the front of the church."

June 26, 1955 -- "The church voted to raise the pastor's salary from $35.00 to $40.00 each Sunday if the offering exceeds $40.00 after expenses have been paid."

July 24, 1955 -- "The church voted to have a bar-b-q. Bill McDuffie was appointed to be in charge of the Bar-b-q committee and Mrs. Doris Calhoun to act as side dressing committee." (The church had a bar-b-q annually each Labor Day.) "The church voted to have a singing school the last of August. Harold Littlejohn, Alvin Stephenson, and Joe Louis Johnson were appointed as a planning committee for it."

August 14, 1955 -- "The church election was held and the following were elected: Reverend A.I. Bowman, pastor..."

October 23, 1955 -- It was recommended to the church by the board of deacons that 10% of the combined total of the Sunday School offering and the church offering be given to the Cooperative Program. "It was moved and seconded to give 10% of the church and Sunday School offering to the Cooperative Program."

November 27, 1955 -- "Plans for the Sunday School rooms were presented to and accepted by the church. A finance committee was appointed by the pastor. The following were appointed: Buster Pritchett, chairman; James Johnson, Edd Johnson, and Eugene Angel. A move was made and passed to take pledges. A total of $2475.00 was pledged. It was moved and passed that the money in the church treasury be used on the Sunday School building."

January 22, 1956 -- "I.A. Clark and Clytus Angel were elected to be in charge of building the Sunday School rooms."

July 23, 1956 -- "An open letter of resignation was read by the pastor, the Reverend Albert I. Bowman. Motion was made and seconded to accept the resignation."

September 23, 1956 -- "The church voted to have only Sunday School on the fifth Sunday and to have an intermission between Sunday School and church."

October 28, 1956 -- "The Reverend Hillary Johnson was elected to serve as pastor for the coming year."

February 24, 1957 -- "The W.M.U. will meet each first Tuesday night. The officers elected were approved by the church."

March 24, 1956 -- "Motion was made, seconded, and passed for the Sunday School treasurer to run over to the finance committee all surplus funds until the building program is completed. A committee was appointed to nominate officers for a man's Brotherhood group."

July 28, 1957 -- "Motion was made, seconded, and passed to organize a Royal Ambassador group."

August 25, 1957 -- Reverend Hillary Johnson was re-elected as pastor by the church.

January 26, 1957 -- The church voted to "set up a fund for building a pastor's home in the future."

March 30, 1958 -- "Mrs. Angel and Mrs. Nita Angel were appointed to be in charge of the cradle roll."

April 27, 1958 -- "Motion was made and passed to build concrete tables. Clytus Angel was elected to have them built. Tables are to be built in the old driveway. Clytus Angel, G.W. Angel, and Bill McDuffie were appointed on a planning committee to build an arch."

May 25, 1958 -- The church voted to "pay the expenses of building the tables out of the church treasury. Motion was made and passed for the committee to go ahead and build the arch in the church. Motion was made and passed to buy new song books."

October 26, 1958 -- The church voted to put one color of tile on the church floor. A committee of Doyle Pritchett, Tom Angel, and James Johnson were appointed to get prices for the flooring.

November 23, 1958 -- "The board of deacons recommended that the church elect three new deacons. Motion was made, seconded, and passed to do this. Two weeks from this date each member is requested to bring a list of five men and the three men named the most times will be elected."

April 1, 1959 -- "Motion was made, seconded, and passed to accept the clock from Sterling Jewelers." (The clock hung in the rear of the church for over 25 years.)

September 6, 1959 -- The church voted for the "housekeeper to light the heaters during the cold month, for which extra pay will be given...Motion was made, seconded, and passed to accept Reverend Hillary Johnson's resignation as pastor...A unanimous vote of commendation was given to Reverend Hillary G. Johnson by the church."

January 3, 1960 -- "The board of deacons acting as a pulpit committee recommended and nominated Reverend Oscar Mitchell for pastor. Motion was made, seconded, and passed that nominations be closed. Reverend Oscar Mitchell was elected by the church."

May 1, 1960 -- The church voted "to let the Brotherhood put lights outside the church. The lights to be paid for by the church."

June 6, 1960 -- The church voted to "either buy or build a pastorium." It was voted to "buy Alvin Stephenson's house." Edd Johnson, Charles Calhoun, and Will S. Prickett were appointed to a finance committee. Miss Louise Angel served as the secretary. The church voted to "transfer from each church department all money possible to the pastorium fund."

August 14, 1960 -- The church voted "for the pastor to appoint a committee to borrow money to buy the pastorium."

April 1, 1962 -- "Motion was made, seconded, and passed not to count anyone absent from Sunday School and church for up to three weeks when they are away, if the attend Sunday School and church where they are."

June 3, 1962 -- The church voted to "help pay the hospital chaplain's salary. The church voted to give $5.00 each month...Motion was made, seconded, and passed to insure the church building and contents. The board of deacons is to set the amount. The board of deacons recommended that the money be transferred from each department treasury to the pastorium fund by the next due date to help pay off the note."

May 5, 1963 -- The church voted "to have a well drilled. The cost to be $600.00 including the pump."

June 2, 1963 -- "The Reverend Walker Dean was nominated by the board of deacons for pastor and elected by the church."

July 7, 1963 -- "Motion was made, seconded, and passed to buy a drinking fountain to be paid for out of the church treasury."

August 4, 1963 -- "The annual fellowship will be held on Labor Day, as usual."

December 1, 1963 -- "It was recommended by the Board of Deacons that the church go on a church budget"...The church appointed a committee to study the recommendation. Appointed were: Clytus Angel, Harold Littlejohn, and Alvin Stephenson.

January 19, 1964 -- "A letter of resignation was read by the pastor effective February 16, 1964."

March 1, 1964 -- "The church voted to go on a church budget. The church voted to accept the budget drawn up by the committee."

October 4, 1964 -- The board of deacons recommended the Reverend Henry Harris for pastor for the coming year at a salary of $75.00 per week."

May 2, 1965 -- "The board of deacons recommended that the Sunday School annex roof be fixed and that the church be insulated. Motion was made and passed that the recommendation be accepted."

June 6, 1965 -- "Clytus Angel was commended by the church for his prompt action in repairing the church annex roof."

July 4, 1965 -- The trustees were allowed "to spend up to $50.00 without the approval of the church."

November 7, 1965 -- The treasurer was authorized "to place all funds in excess of $500.00 on savings until needed by the church."

January 2, 1966 -- "Motion was made, seconded, and passed to buy rugs to cover the nursery floor. Appointed on a committee to do this were: Mary Frances Hyde, Edd Johnson, and Carolyn Burgess."

February 6, 1966 - The rug committee was instructed to "buy additional rugs to go in the Primary and Beginners class rooms."

September 4, 1966 -- "Edd Johnson gave a brief report on Brother McComb. The board of deacons recommended Brother McComb as pastor and placed him in nomination. Brother McComb was elected without a dissenting vote. The board of deacons recommended that the pastor's salary be $100.00 per week with $10.00 per week expense money. The church voted to accept the recommendations."

December 11, 1966 -- "The board of deacons recommended that the business session be held on Sunday night for one quarter."

February 19, 1967 -- The church voted "to accept the pastor's resignation as given the first Sunday of February to be effective 30 days later."

June 11, 1967 -- Reverend Don Ledbetter was recommended to the church as pastor. "A vote was called for." Reverend Ledbette was called as pastor.

July 19, 1967 -- The church voted to "buy the paint for the W.M.U. to paint the church."

August 6, 1967 -- "Motion was made and passed to have the annual Labor Day picnic."

September 3, 1967 -- "The board of deacons recommended that the church fix a new entrance to the auditorium, panel the walls, install new windows, and pews. Motion was made and passed to do this. It was also recommended to elect three new deacons...Earl Lockett was appointed to accept offers to buy memorial windows and pews...The Board of Deacons recommended that the church go full time and pay the pastor $100.00 per week plus $10.00 per week car expense."

December 3, 1967 -- "Motion was made and passed approving as new deacons Earl Lockett, Alvin Stephenson, and Roscoe Angel."

April 7, 1968 -- "Motion was made and passed to install wall-to-wall carpet in the church."

July 7, 1968 -- "A motion was made and passed to appoint a committee to look into prices to install air conditioning in the church."

August 11, 1968 -- "Motion was made, seconded, and passed to accept pledges for the cooling and heating system for the church and the pledges to be in by the following Sunday."

September 15, 1968 -- "The W.M.U. asked the help of the people of the church to help support financially a project they have undertaken of sending Christmas boxes to the boys of our church that are in the service of our country."

October 6, 1968 -- "After a testimony by Terry Johnson, a motion was made and passed that he be licensed to preach by the church."

February 2, 1969 -- "Motion was made and seconded that Stanley Pritchett be licensed to preach. The motion carried."

June 8, 1969 -- "Motion was made and passed that the parking area around the church be blacktopped at the expense of $965.00. Motion was made and passed that the pastor be sent to New Orleans to the Southern Baptist Convention."

September 7, 1969 -- "Motion was made and seconded to accept the pastor's resignation." (Don Ledbetter resigned.)

November 9, 1969 -- "Motion was made and passed that the church have the pastorium appraised and to see what it would cost to sell it and build a new pastorium. The church voted to elect a new pastor. Brother Dorris Wade was placed in nomination and elected."

January 4, 1970 -- "The pastor appointed a building committee made up of Clytus Angel, chairman; Marshall Prickett, and Doug Pritchett. Motion was made, seconded, and passed that the building committee buy and install a pump for the church well."

February 8, 1970 -- The church accepted "the recommendation of the building committee to sell the old pastorium for $6100.00 and build a new one."

April 12, 1970 -- The church voted "to buy an organ and that Brother Wade take care of the details."

September 13, 1970 -- "It was recommended to the church by the Sunday School superintendent that the large room upstairs be used for morning devotionals by the young people and that the church buy a piano for the room... Brother Wade and Alvin Stephenson were appointed as a committee to buy a piano."

October 4, 1970 -- The church voted to "buy the piano for $650.00."

October 2, 1971 -- A motion passed "to keep the nursery open during the worship hour for children up to two years old."

May 14, 1972 -- "Today's special conference was called for the purpose of discussing the building of a playground on the church property. Motion was made and passed that the pastor appoint a committee of older and younger people, with him as chairman. to take care of the plans. Appointed on the committee were: Gary Angel, Eddie Johnson, Alvin Stephenson, and Will S. Prickett. Motion was made and passed that the church will help the young people with the financing of the tennis court and playground."

August 6, 1972 -- The church voted to get a new steeple for the church. Brother Wade appointed "Clytus Angel, Jim Hyde, and Marshall Prickett to see abut the steeple. It was suggested that the old steeple be torn down and the roof patched until the new steeple can be obtained."

September 3, 1972 -- The church voted to "pay in retirement for the pastor and to increase his travel expense to $10.00 per week."

February 4, 1973 -- "A motion was made and passed that a committee be appointed to make plans for a fellowship hall. Appointed were: Marshall Prickett, chairman; Joyce Tillison, Nita Angel, Alvin Stephenson, and Roscoe Angel."

March 4, 1973 -- "It was recommended by the fellowship hall committee that a building 28' by 48' of brick and block be build at an approximate cost of $12,408.00."

April 1, 1973 -- "Appointed on the building committee were: Winston Wilson, chairman; Don Carroll, Stanley Pritchett, Mike Johnson, and Clytus Angel."

April 1, 1973 -- "The building committee asked for permission to brick the fellowship hall from the ground up." Permission was granted. The committee was also given authority to finish the tennis court.

September 2, 1973 -- "The deacon board recommended that a youth director be employed...Appointed on a committee to secure a youth director were: Reverend D.D. Wade, chairman; Alvin Stephenson, Mike Johnson, and Mrs. Geraldine Prickett.

September, 1973 -- (Allen Haynes was elected as youth director.)

March 3, 1974 -- The church voted "to buy drapes for the fellowship hall."

August 4, 1974 -- "It was recommended by the board of deacons that Stanley and Judy Pritchett serve as temporary youth directors" after the resignation of Allen Haynes.

August 4, 1974 -- "Motion was made and passed that Allen Haynes be licensed to preach."

September 8, 1974 -- It was recommended by the budget committee to raise the price of wreaths sent by the church from $10.00 to $15.00 and to send a bucket of fried chicken to homes where a death has occurred.

December 29, 1974 -- "Brother David Allen Haynes was ordained to the ministry by the church on this date."

February 1975 -- (Tim Cochran was elected as youth director.)

May 4, 1975 -- "Motion was made and passed to drop the ceiling in the auditorium and to install new light fixtures."

November 2, 1975 -- "Today the pastor, Reverend D.D. Wade, resigned, effective thirty days from today."

March 21, 1976 -- "Reverend Dan Phillips was recommended and placed in nomination by the pulpit committee. Motion was made and passed that the nominations be closed." Reverend Phillips was called as pastor.

May 9, 1976 -- The church voted to "recommend Tim Cochran to the seminary."

July 11, 1976 -- "Brother Tim Cochran resigned as youth director of the church."

August 15, 1976 -- "Upon recommendation of the brotherhood, motion was made and seconded that one of the rooms in the Sunday School section be made into a pastor's study. The motion carried. The pastor appointed a committee made up of Jan Calhoun, Alvin Stephenson, and Marshall Prickett to study the need, find the cost, and make a recommendation about a P.A. system for the church."

September 5, 1976 -- "Motion was made to get the church treated for termites." (The recommendation was made after termites had swarmed during the Sunday morning service.)

October 24, 1976 -- "The nominating committee recommended and placed in nomination Doug Gregory for youth director. The church approved the recommendation."

December 5, 1976 -- "By consent, the church agreed to accept a new organ from an anonymous giver."

January 2, 1977 -- "Motion was made and passed that a local missions committee be appointed, made up of the pastor and one member each from the Brotherhood and the W.M.U."

February 13, 1977 -- "The board of deacons recommended and moved to grant Marion Clark's request that he be removed from the board of deacons. The motion carried."

April 3, 1977 -- "The Local Missions Committee reported that...$100.00 had been given to the Cerebral Palsy building fund" (to complete a building for their center.)

May 1, 1977 -- The church established a "Hospitality Committee to welcome new residents into our community. Doris Prickett was appointed chairman. Members appointed later were Gladys Angel and Will S. Prickett."

June 5, 1977 -- "Doug Gregory resigned, effective June 26."

December 11, 1977 -- "The committee to find a youth director recommended to the church David Freeman. The church voted...in favor of the recommendation."

December 3, 1978 -- "It was recommended by the deacon board and made in the form of a motion that Brother Tommy Reaves be the interim pastor. The motion carried." The church voted "to give the deacons the authority to appoint a pulpit committee."

January 7, 1979 -- The Brotherhood recommended "that the church purchase a school bus for the use of the church. The motion carried."

March 11, 1979 -- "The deacon board recommended that Earl and Laura Lockett work with the youth of the church temporarily while seeking a youth director."

September 2, 1979 -- "The committee on the fellowship hall recommended that the water getting in be stopped and that it would take $3200.00 to complete the building...Motion was made to install a telephone in the church building...The pulpit committee recommended to the church Reverend Tommy Reaves for pastor..." All recommendations were approved by the church.

October 7, 1979 -- "The church voted to pay $2800.00 for the church bus."

December 2, 1979 -- "It was suggested to incorporate in the church minutes names of persons joining the church by baptism, letter, or statement. After a discussion, the church voted to purchase the sound system for $500.00. The board of deacons recommended that the outside of the church be painted, repairs to nursery be made, improvements be made to the general appearance of the church, improve the lighting of the church, and purchase new song books..." The motions passed. "Motion was made and passed to check on new carpet for the church and pads for the pews." The committee responsible for the upgrading of appearance were: Marshall Prickett, Roscoe Angel, and Lloyd Fike.

January 6, 1980 -- The deacon board recommended that Lloyd Fike, Willard Ray, and Earl Lockett, being ordained deacons, serve on the deacon board." (They had joined Angel Grove from other churches.)

February 3, 1980 -- The church voted "to buy pulpit chairs...Appointed to work with the pastor in choosing them were Clayton Johnson and Don Carroll."

March, 1980 -- (Gary Smith was elected at youth director.)

April, 1980 -- "The church voted "to license Earl Lockett to preach...Motion was made and passed to recommend Earl to enter seminary...It was recommended by the board of deacons that: the church start a weekly newsletter and hire someone part-time to help get it out...That the volleyball court be refinished...That the pastor appoint a committee to plan a baptistry and to enlarge the Sunday School rooms." All recommendations were approved by the church.

May 4, 1980 -- Reverend Tommy Reaves "read a letter of resignation to the church effective May 25, 1980."

July 6, 1980 -- Reverend G.D. Waites was recommended "by the pulpit committee as interim pastor."

November 2, 1980 -- "Motion was made to elect three additional deacons at the next regular meeting."

December 14, 1980 -- A report was given by James Hobbs for the long-range planning committee. The church voted to "start a building fund with $5000.00 of the money on hand...The suggestion of immediate need was to construct a 32' x 45' wing consisting of 6 rooms upstairs and 6 rooms downstairs at approximately $28,000.00, with labor participation from the members. Extend the auditorium, tear out the vestibule, glass in the front porch, and paint the church white. After some discussion, it was decided to elect 4 deacons instead of three as earlier passed. Elected were: John Burns, Don Carroll, Jackie Johnson, and Rodney Young." The church voted to "install heating and cooling in the pastorium at a cost of about $3000.00. Motion was made and carried to pay for Reverend Waites a hearing aid for Christmas..."

January 4, 1981 -- Lloyd Fike was placed in charge of the church's tape ministry." A letter of resignation was read from Gary Smith, youth director, effective February 1st.

February 1, 1981 -- "James Hobbs reported for the Planning Committee that they recommended that the church set aside a day or every 5th Sunday as a time to give to the building fund and also that a day to make pledges be set."

March 1, 1981 -- The church voted to "buy 4 tables and 30 chairs for the fellowship hall...install some supports in the fellowship hall. Motion was made and seconded to call Brother Wayne Fain as pastor." The motion carried.

July 5, 1981 -- The church decided to "accept loans from church members at the current interest rate for money market CD's as alternative source of funds" to pay for construction of the new addition.

February 7, 1982 -- "It was recommended by the deacon board that Earl Lockett be approved for admittance to the New Orleans Baptist Theological Seminary." The church voted to do so.

April 4, 1982 -- "It was recommended by the Building Committee to pave the parking lot including the basketball court, landscape the grounds, enlarge the sanctuary, and finish the men's rest room." The motion carried.

August 22, 1982 -- "Glen Bonds was elected as youth director."

November 6, 1982 -- The budget committee recommended that the flower allotment for wreaths be raised from $25.00 to $50.00. (Wreaths are sent to families when deaths occur.)

February 12, 1984 -- The deacon board recommended "that a church secretary be hired...and that the Sunday School and Training Union rolls be reviewed every six months and those not being in attendance during this period, be removed from the rolls." The recommendations passed.

April 8, 1984 -- "The nominating committee reported to the church that it would like to recommend Mrs. Ann Cockley for church secretary...The motion carried."

June 17, 1984 -- "Motion was made to ring the bell to end Sunday School at twenty minutes until eleven o'clock a.m. and to ring the bell to end Training Union at 6:20 p.m. Morning worship services to start at 10:50 a.m. and evening services to start at 6:30 p.m. The motion carried."

August 5, 1984 -- "Motion was made, seconded, and passed to approve an application for admission to the New Orleans Baptist Theological Seminary for Glen Bonds."

September 16, 1984 -- "The pulpit committee recommended Brother Mark Owen for interim pastor."

November 4, 1984 -- "A proposal was made to study the feasibility of installing a covered area at the church to unload under during rainy weather. Motion was made, seconded, and passed that the building committee take care of this and report back to the church."

January 6, 1985 -- The deacon board recommended the following items: Replace the roofs on the fellowship hall and parsonage. Paint the Sunday School rooms and install guard rails on the walls. They announced that Roscoe Angel has requested t be put on the deacon inactive list." Each of the recommendations was passed by the church.

February 3, 1985 -- "The pulpit committee recommended Brother Eugene Burgess for pastor and made a motion that this recommendation be accepted...The motion was seconded and passed with a unanimous vote...The Building Committee recommended that we install a dishwasher in the pastorium and install drapes." These motions passed.

March 3, 1985 -- "The deacon board recommended that the church, in the near future, elect and ordain three new deacons."

May 5, 1985 -- "Paul Brown was recommended for youth director." He was elected by the church. "The deacon board recommended ...that Brother Gene Burgess be authorized to purchase a used or new riding lawn mower."

June 2, 1985 -- "The deacon board announced that: Paul Clark, Eddie Johnson, and Bill Miller were elected as the new deacons. They also announced that all deacon board officers will be put on a yearly rotating basis.

August 4, 1985 -- The church voted to purchase a new copier. The deacon board recommended "that Curtis Johnson's request to be put on the inactive deacon list be honored. The church voted to honor his request...The church was asked to think about a new bus and a new organ for the church."

September 15, 1985 -- The Budget Committee recommended to the church that the budget be expended for a total of fifteen months, and then for the budget "to run from January 1 to December 31 each year...The Budget Committee also recommended to the church a change in the percentage of church funds given to missions. It was recommended and made in the form of a motion that 6% be given to the Cooperative Program and 6% be given to the Associational Missions Program." Both recommendations were accepted by the church.

October 6, 1985 -- "The pastor commended Carrial Crittenden for making furniture for the pre-school department"...Alvin

Stephenson, Becky Craven, and the pastor were recommended to find a church pianist.

December 1, 1985 -- "Paul Brown read a letter of resignation to the church," (giving up his position as youth director.)

March 3, 1986 -- James Hobbs, Danny Craven, James Johnson, and Bill Miller were selected to be on an "Advisory Committee to obtain all the information on transportation options available to use, along with financing information, if necessary, and prices."

April 13, 1986 -- It was reported that the WMU and the Brotherhood held a bike-a-thon together. (The bike-a-thon gave children an opportunity to ride their bikes to raise money for the Annie Armstrong offering.)

April 13, 1986 -- "James Johnson reported that the Transportation Committee had been meeting. They have looked at several vehicles, but have not reached any consensus of opinion yet. They will be looking at more vehicles in the near future." Nine members of the BALL group went to the nursing home and delivered 200 bananas. (The BALL group is the "Be Active Live Longer senior adult group.)

May 4, 1986 -- "The Transportation Committee recommended, in the form of a motion that we purchase...a 29-passenger bus at a cost of $38,487.00, delivered...The motion was put to a vote and carried...The deacons recommended that in the future any major decision to be voted on be put on an agenda and given to the members prior to the meeting."

July 6, 1986 -- "The Brotherhood reported that a refrigerator had been donated for the food closet."

October 5, 1986 -- "Vendala has been asked to cater the meal at the associational meeting to be held at our church...Will S. Prickett, chairman of the Music/Youth Director Search Committee, recommended in the form of a motion that Dee Ingram be called as Youth/Music Director. It was seconded and carried unanimously."

December 7, 1986 -- A motion was made "that we allocate $6000.000 for" renovation of the fellowship hall to include new lights and ceiling and a heating and air conditioning unit so that the basement could be used for various activities. It was also reported that the old church bus was given to Pleasant Valley Baptist Church.

January 4, 1987 -- With Don Carroll acting as moderator...The Pastor made a motion that Angel Grove become the sponsor of the Owens sisters currently confined to the nursing home. We would pay their medicine and laundry bills. The motion was carried. "We will extend this to anyone who is a member of our church who has no one else to be responsible for them..."

January 4, 1987 -- "The Pastor made a motion that we establish a trust fund to help defray the cost of a liver transplant for Diane Johnson, should it become necessary." The motion passed.

January 11, 1987 -- "The total operating budget is $73,995.00, and with 15% added for missions, the total is $85,684.25."

April 5, 1987 -- A motion was made "that we set aside three parking spaces at the side of the church for the handicapped and three spaces in the front for visitors." The motion was carried.

May 3, 1987 -- A motion was made by the long-range planning committee "to move the volleyball court behind the fellowship hall and remove the picnic tables" for additional parking space. After some discussion, the church voted to leave the picnic tables and only move the volleyball court.

August 2, 1987 -- A motion was made "that we incorporate Angel Grove Baptist Church." After some discussion "the vote was taken and the results were 39 for and 10 against. The motion carried."

October 4, 1987 -- "Dee Ingram then tendered his resignation as Music/Youth Director..."

October 25, 1987 -- A motion was made "that the church call Wayne Dozier as interim Music/Youth Director through December, 1987." The motion carried.

November 8, 1987 -- "The Pastor reported that the fellowship hall renovation is nearly completed. Ceiling tiles and lights have been added to the basement and new lights to the kitchen area. Mr. and Mrs. Bromcock from Centre, Alabama have donated their time to do the wiring for the lights.

November 15, 1987 -- "The resolution...for incorporation of Angel Grove Baptist Church was read by the church clerk. A motion was made...and passed that the trustees complete the incorporation."

January 10, 1988 -- "A motion was made...that David and Sharon Shaw work with the youth under the direction and training of Wayne Dozier." The motion carried.

January 10, 1988 -- The new church budget "reflects a new item of insurance on the Pastor's household belongings."

March 6, 1988 -- A motion was made "that the kitchen floor in the pastorium and the utility room be repaired...It was amended to add carpet to the dining room area." The motion carried.

Mr. I.A. Clark & Mr. F.T. Angel
Two who served our country during WW I and later served as deacons.

Mr. Smith Moore served our country during WW I.
He was a member of our church

PASTORS

The first pastor of Angel Grove Baptist Church was Mr. H.L. (Hughes) Johnston. He was pastor from 1888 until 1892, and from 1893 until 1901. Reverend Johnston was born on May 13, 1851. He married Narmesia S. Lanford and was the father of seven children. Reverend Johnston was ordained May, 1878 at Post Oak Baptist Church and spent 40 years in the ministry. He died March 13, 1919.

Rev. & Mrs. H.L. Johnston with pig.

Rev. Mrs. G.S. Boozer

In 1892 G.S. Boozer was pastor, and again from 1902 until 1907. Reverend Boozer was born on December 22, 1847 and was ordained on November 28, 1886 at Baptist Church of Christ at Liberty Coosa. He spent approximately 22 years in the ministry. G.S. Boozer was married to the former Rebecca Narcissus and they had three children; Henry Teague Boozer, Edward Lee Boozer, and Loula Annie Boozer Atkins. He was a farmer as well as a preacher. It is believed that he served with the Confederate army in Co.A, 51st, Alabama Partisan Rangers. Reverend Boozer died on May 25, 1908 and is buried in Thomas Cemetery near Jacksonville.

T.A. Smith
1909

T. A. Smith pastored Angel in 1909. He was one of four men who met as a presbytery to take into consideration the gifts and qualifications of Brother Gillum S. Boozer, to set him (Brother Boozer) apart to the full work of the ministry. This was done in Etowah County, from a call made by the Baptist Church of Christ at Liberty Coosa, on the 28th of November, 1886.

The men were:

M. A. Cornelious
R.S. Steel
T.A. Smith
H.R. Culberson

Rev. & Mrs. S.H. Carr

From 1911 to 1912 Reverend Sidney H. Carr came to pastor Angel Grove. Reverend Carr was born on November 11, 1877 in Texas, but spent his childhood in the West Point community. He lived in the area the rest of his life and died there May 6, 1951. During his lifetime he preached for 30 years. Two of these years, 1911 and 1912, were spent at Angel Grove. He was also pastor at Walnut Springs, which was located near Boozer Lake in the West Point community before the existence of West Point Baptist Church. Reverend Carr was married to the former Mary Holden and they had five children.

Rev. & Mrs. E.J. Clark

During the year 1913, the Reverend Eddie J. Clark pastored at Angel. He was born in this community on November 20, 1880 and lived here all of his life except for two or three years spent in Texas. He was ordained in 1906 at Angel Grove and spent approximately fifty years preaching, while serving four churches. Mr. Clark married the former Addie Lanford. They had five children. He also served as assistant pastor in the 1930's. At this time we had Saturday morning services once a month, which he preached.

T. F. McCULLOUGH

Reverend Thomas Franklin McCullough served Angel Grove Baptist Church as pastor from 1914 to 1917. He was born in 1860 and he and his wife, Mrs. Nancy Jane McCullough, lived at North Pelham Road in Jacksonville, Alabama. There they reared a family of several children plus one adopted child, Ruby Ann Parsons. Reverend McCullough preached at Angel Grove Church each third Sunday of the month. He also served at other area churches. The McCullough family were active members of the First Baptist Church, Jacksonville, Alabama. Thomas McCullough died in 1942

and he and Mrs. McCullough, along with several family members, are buried in the Jacksonville City Cemetery. A daughter, Mrs. Itasca Sturkie, is a nursing home patient in Tuscaloosa. Alabama.

Rev. Noah Stephens

Reverend Noah Stephens pastored Angel from 1918 until 1920 and preached on the second Sunday of each month. Reverend Stephens was born August 23, 1956 in Calhoun County, Alabama. He was married to Elizabeth Post and they had 2 sons and 3 daughters. Mrs. Stephens died October 5, 1894 at the age of 33. Reverend Stephens later married again and had three more sons. After approximately 40 years of preaching in and around Calhoun County, Reverend Stephens died February 11, 1922 at the age of 66. He was pastor at Blue Mountain Baptist Church at this time.

Rev. & Mrs. G.S. Morris

Pastor at Angel from 1921 until 1928 was the Reverend G.S. Morris. He was born October 9, 1892. He spent fifty-one years in the ministry and served thirty-two churches. He served as pastor of sixteen churches in Calhoun County. He served as moderator of the Calhoun Association for two years. He was pastor at Angel during the time of one service-a-month. At this time he served four churches as pastor. One of the highlights of his pastorate was after a revival in 1928, there was twenty-eight people baptized. His records show that in his years of pastoring that he baptized more than 3,000 and conducted over 500 funerals and performed more than 300 weddings. Brother Morris was educated in one our Baptist Academies. He led in building the first pastorium and Sunday School rooms in the rural areas. Reverend Morris's wife's name was Mary, and they had eight children. On October 8, 1960, just one day short of his 68th birthday, Reverend Morris died.

53

Rev. & Mrs. W.H. Harris

In 1931 a man who became one of Angel's oldest and dearest friends came as Pastor, the Reverend Henry Harris. Brother Harris was born March 29, 1905. He was licensed to preach at Greensport Baptist Church in St. Clair County in 1923. Reverend Harris was ordained in March 1925 at First Baptist Church of Cave Springs, Georgia. He spent 65 years preaching the gospel in twenty-one churches, nineteen in Alabama and two in Georgia. He served at Angel from 1931-1937, 1946-1949, and 1964-65.

During his first pastorate, he served two other churches and was a full time school teacher.

One of his major accomplishments during his first pastorate at Angel, he felt, was his semi-getting the church back together. During his second pastorate we built our present church building in 1947.

Reverend Harris was a graduate of Howard College and Jacksonville State Teachers College. He also served seven years in the U.S. Army as a Chaplain. He served from 1942-1946 and 1953-1957. His time in the military was spent in the United States, France, and Korea. He was also a Mason.

Reverend Harris's wife's maiden name is Willie E. Dunn, and they had five children, four still living and one deceased. Brother Harris died on November 29, 1987.

54

From 1938-1941 Angel Grove was pastored by Brother Leslie Hall, born on February 22, 1910. He was ordained at Pilgram's Rest Baptist Church in Gadsden, Alabama in 1937. He served five churches in his twenty-five years in the ministry. His wife was the former Fannie Johnson, who survives him. They had three children. His wife states that they enjoyed the years spent in our church and the fellowship. It was during Reverend Hall's pastorate that the church voted to build a new church, which is our present building. On July 20, 1964, Reverend Leslie Hall died.

Rev. Leslie Hall

Rev. Emmett Boozer

In September of 1941, Reverend Henry Emmett Boozer came to pastor Angel Grove. He was born in the Williams Community to Edward Lee and Sallie Vaughn Boozer. He preached his first message on Christmas Eve day in 1922 and was ordained in September of 1923 at Williams Church. He spent 35 years preaching the gospel, serving nine churches - Pleasant Valley, Angel, West Point, Mt. Gilead, Williams, New Liberty, Hopewell, Asberry, and Nance's Creek.

Reverend Boozer was married to the former Sallie Mae Glass and they had two sons, Harold Wilson Boozer (deceased) and Thomas Edsel Boozer of Marietta, Georgia. Mrs. Boozer related that "he enjoyed the cooperation of folk and the love shared and shown while at Angel. His highlight at Angel was being able to set aside a certain percent of his income to help start and build a new building at Angel Church." She said she was "glad" when he told her he was called to preach. "The Lord had talked to him for a while," she said. He got sick and Preacher Boozer said to her, "The Lord means business, I've got to preach." Reverend Boozer died on April 15, 1958 and is buried in Williams (Ohatchee) Cemetery.

The Reverend Fred Curvin was pastor from 1950-1953. He was born August 30, 1921. He was ordained at Mt. Zion Baptist Church in Alexandria, Alabama in 1949, and spent the next 32 years preaching. During that time he served seven churches. He attended Howard College for two years. He and his wife, the former Mable Cagle, had two children. While Reverend Curvin was at Angel our first B.T.U. began to meet every Sunday. On May 24, 1980 Reverend Curvin died.

Rev. & Mrs. Fred Curvin

Rev. George Vines

Reverend George Vines was born August 20, 1927, and was married to Mary C. Turner. He was the father of one child. Reverend Vines was ordained to the ministry on January 21, 1945 in Pensacola, Florida. He then spent the next 44 years in the ministry, and served seven churches. One of those years, 1953, was at Angel Grove. He attended Howard College for three years. He says his most memorable experience at Angel was "the first sermon I delivered there." He feels God has used and will use Angel Grove.

Rev. Albert Bowman

Brother Albert Bowman was born April 15, 1929. He was ordained at Blue Mountain Baptist Church, Anniston, Alabama by Reverend Buford Johnson. He has been preaching thirty-five years and has served ten churches and two missions in Alabama, California, and Texas. He served Angel Grove from 1954-1956.

It was during his pastorate that the church started giving 10 percent to the Cooperative Program and other missions. He states that "Angel was his first church and will always be very special. We were very young (26 years) and made lots of mistakes. He is currently pastor of a church in Hewitt, Texas. It was during his pastorate that a front was built on our church and Sunday School rooms added.

He states that his most memorable experience at Angel was: "one Sunday morning when my wife was playing the piano a large chicken snake was seen on the picture above the piano. We didn't stop singing. After the song was over, Clytus Angel snatched it and ran out the back door."

His wife is the former Dorothy Garrett. They have five children and nine grandchildren.

Rev. Hillary Johnson

The pastor of Angel Grove Church from 1956-1960 was Brother Hillary Johnson. He was born January 17, 1900. He was ordained on February 11, 1945 at First Baptist Church, Gadsden, Alabama. During the next twenty-four years he served six churches. He attended Howard College, which is now Samford University. His wife, the former Minnie Cooper, survives him. She is a nursing home resident. They have three children.

It was during Brother Johnson's pastorate that we organized our first Brotherhood and RA organization. Our concrete picnic table was built and an arch was put in the church. Also a Cradle Roll was started for babies in our church. Brother Hillary Johnson died on May 25, 1969.

From 1960-1963 Reverend Oscar Mitchell was the pastor. He was born on February 12, 1914. His ordination took place at Odenville Baptist Church on April 23, 1944. He spent forty-one years preaching and pastored several churches. His formal education included a B.S. degree from Jacksonville State Teachers College, and ministerial courses at Samford University. His wife is the former Nellie Whited, and they had three children.

Our first pastorium was purchased and paid for during Brother Mitchell's pastorate.

Mrs. Mitchell writes concerning their most memorable experience, "the love and closeness that everyone felt for each other. I especially remember how nice the young people were and how we enjoyed them coming to our home. The Christmas tree at church where everyone gave each other small gifts and it was decorated with hankerchiefs. We never pastored a church that we felt closer to the people than at Angel Grove. Everyone was so good to us. The people were so supportive - we felt like they were a greater blessing to us than we were to them."

Rev. Oscar Mitchell

Rev. Walker Dean

Angel Grove was pastored by Walker Dean in 1963 for a very brief time (6 months). He was born on December 14, 1919 and was ordained at Ruhama Baptist Church in Anniston, Alabama on July 28, 1946. Reverend Dean served ten churches during the next 42 years. His wife is the former Hazel Nowland and they have two children. They now reside in Anniston, Alabama.

Pastor Paul McComb
Sept. 1966 - Feb. 1967

THE REV. PAUL McCOMB

Rev. Don Ledbetter

Reverend Don Ledbetter was born July 3, 1942, accepted Christ in June of 1957, was licensed to preach on November 27, 1966, was ordained June 25, 1967 at Pine Avenue Baptist Church, Anniston, Alabama. He has spent 21 years preaching and has pastored four churches. Angel Grove was his first church to serve, and that was from 1967-1969. The other three were Ebenezer Baptist, Columbia, Alabama; Second Baptist, Columbus, Georgia; and Liberty Baptist, College Park, Georgia. He has served in full time evangelism for four years.

Reverend Ledbetter has Bachelor of Divinity, Master of Ministry, and Doctor of Ministry degrees.

His wife's maiden name was Linda Spears. They have two sons, Steven and Stanley.

Reverend Ledbetter states that his most memorable experience was one Sunday afternoon when nine people were baptized in the creek. He feels that his major accomplishment was helping the church to re-focus on Christ. He states that in the three years that he served Angel, the Lord blessed in many areas. The church grew in numbers and in Spirit. He says, "I remember Angel with love, and praise His name for the good things He did for us.

60

Reverend D. D. Wade was born on September 14, 1914. He attended school at Ohatchee and Alexandria. He is married to Nella Cox Wade and is the father of two children. Preacher Wade was ordained into the ministry on May 5, 1954, at Mt. Zion Baptist Church in Alexandria, Alabama. During his 34 years in the ministry that followed, He served seven churches. One of these was, of course, Angel Grove, and that was from the Fall of 1969 until the Fall of 1975. One of the most memorable experiences during his ministry at Angel was building the new pastorium and the fellowship hall. "The pastorium was paid for in one year," he said. Reverend Wade enjoyed being at Angel Grove and loved all the people.

Rev. & Mrs. Dan Phillips and Melinda

Coming to pastor Angel Grove after Reverend Wade was Reverend Dan Phillips. He was born on October 5, 1943, and was ordained at Walnut Street Baptist Church in Louisville, Kentucky on October 22, 1970. During his seventeen years of pastoring he has served three churches. He received degrees from Tennessee Technological University, B.S.E.E., Cookville, Tennessee; Master of Divinity, Southern Baptist Theological Seminary, Louisville, Kentucky. His wife is the former Janet Honeycutt, and they have one daughter, Melinda.

He states that his most memorable experience at Angel was when "I was preaching on Caleb in the book of Joshua. I shouted out in the sermon that Caleb said, 'Give me that mountain,' in reference to the promised land. When I did so, our daughter Melinda, who was two shouted out from the back of the church, 'Give me that mountain.'"

During his pastorate here he preached a sermon entitled, "The Greatest Gift" which was chosen in 1978 as one of the award winning sermons at the Southern Baptist Pastors Conference in Atlanta, Georgia. It was published in "Award Winning Sermons" by Broadman Press the same year.

He says Angel holds a special place in their hearts. They were serving here when their daughter was adopted. He is presently a telecommunications consultant for the Baptist Sunday School Board in Nashville, Tennessee. He was the first person hired to begin the Baptist Telecommunication Network.

Rev. & Mrs. Tommy Reaves
LeAnne & Brian

When Brother Phillips tendered his resignation from Angel Grove, Reverend Tommy Reaves was called as interim pastor. Then in 1979 he was asked to become the pastor of Angel Grove Baptist Church, which he accepted. He served at Angel until 1980.

Brother Reaves was born January 27, 1940 and was ordained at Oak Ridge Baptist Church in Anniston, Alabama on October 13, 1963. During his twenty-five years pastoring, he has served six churches. He attended Crenshaw University studying industrial management and New Orleans Theological Seminary where he received an Associate Degree in Pastorial Ministry. His wife is the former Judy Newman, and they have two children.

Reverend Reaves has listed several memorable experiences at Angel. They are as follows:

A. Joy of seeing the attendance climb.
B. The church voting to re-carpet the entire church and paint the educational building.
C. Establishing an office for the pastor.
D. A new lighting system for the church.
E. Cushions for the pews
F. Those great fellowship experiences with all the food.

He feels his major accomplishment at Angel was helping Angel Grove members see and believe that they did indeed have a great church. He remarks that, "Whatever I may become or wherever I may go, Angel Grove will have a great part in it. You gave me a chance to prove to myself and others that I indeed did have something to offer. You allowed me to serve at the lowest point in my life. Angel Grove church will always occupy a high place in my heart and prayers. Very few days pass that I don't think of my eighteen months there. I want to see you grow and grow. It's too soon to quit now."

At the present time, he is pastor of Teamon Baptist Church in Griffin, Georgia.

Pastor Wayne Fain

In 1981, Reverend Wayne Fain became the pastor at Angel. He was born on October 21, 1943 in Talladega, Alabama. On May 16, 1970 he was ordained into the ministry at Moore Avenue Baptist Church in Anniston, Alabama. Brother Fain has an extensive formal education to his credit. He holds a Graduate of Theology degree, a Bachelor of Divinity degree, and Master and Doctor of Ministry degrees. He has spent 21 years in the ministry, 3 of them at Angel Grove. Those were the years from 1981 until 1984.

Brother Fain is married to the former Charlene Rogers. He made the following comment about his tenure at Angel: "We could say so much about the educational building, extension of the auditorium, the parking lot, etc., but the main thing was the good spirit we had and the souls that were saved." He added that he would "always be thankful that God allowed me to serve at Angel. We had a great time."

63

C. EUGENE BURGESS

Born: June 14, 1940   Calhoun County
Saved: 1949
Called to Preach: 1959
Surrendered to Ministry: February 21, 1971

Married 1958 to Carolyn Annette Howard
Children: Gena Burgess St. John
           Timothy Wayne Burgess
           Angela Denise Burgess

Churches Served:
Boiling Springs	Ohatchee, AL	May 1971 – September 1973
South Gadsden	Gadsden, AL	September 1973 – February 1981
Pine Grove	Centre, AL	February 1981 – March 1985
Angel Grove	Jacksonville, AL	March 1985 –

Since becoming pastor of Angel Grove, I have seen the church grow spiritually and physically. There have been a total of 50 additions to the church membership in these 37 months. As the community grows, the prospect for future church growth gets brighter. I would like to express my thanks to the church membership in calling me to be their pastor.

DEACONS

1920	H. E. Wynn Willie Lankford Lee Gardner S.T. Moore H.W. Propst W.F. Turk J.P. McKeown (letter)	1951	Doyle Pritchett Harold Littlejohn Curtis Johnson Clytus Angel
1925	W.H. Angel F.T. Angel I.A. Clark	1959	Marion Clark Edd Johnson Charles Calhoun
1927	F.R. Mullino (letter) T.R. Bryant W.O. Vineyard (letter)	1967	Earl Lockett Alvin Stephenson Roscoe Angel
1937	Clyde Brittain Samuel Wilson Robert Clark Lester Bryant (letter)	1980	Lloyd Fike (letter) Willard Ray (letter) John Burns Don Carroll Jackie Johnson Rodney Young
1942	Mose Prickett Robert Johnson Jack McDuffie	1985	Eddie Johnson Bill Miller Paul Clark

The Present Deacons of Angel Grove
Paul Clark, Carrial Crittenden, Lloyd Fike, Don
Carroll, Rodney Young, Jackie Johnson, Bill Miller,
Clytus Angel, John Burns, Eddie Johnson, Alvin
Stephenson

CHURCH CLERKS

1892	R. J. Angel		1931	T. R. Bryant
1893	R. J. Angel		1931	W. O Vineyard
1894-	(D. B. Johnson		1933	Swindall Weaver
	(E. H. Propes		1935	A. L. Weaver
	(S. P. Usry			
	(G. W. Moore		1937	Samuel Wilson
1919	(S. T. Moore		1938	Curtis Johnson
1920	S. S. Moore		1940	Harold Smith
1921	W. B. Lankford		1942	Hubert Boozer
1923	A. L. Weaver		1948	Clytus Angel
1925	Roscoe Wilson		1954	Will S. Prickett
1926	A. L. Weaver		1986	Pat Miller

R.J. Angel

Curtis Johnson

T.R. Bryant

Hubert Boozer

Will Smith Prickett

Pat Miller

Southern
Baptist
Convention

EASTER MORNING SERVICES   1988

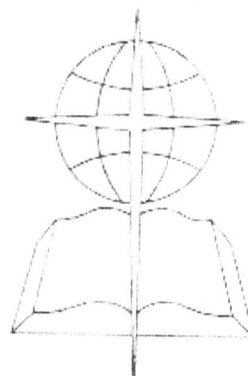

Mrs. R.J. Angel

F.T. Angel

G.W. Angel

Clytus Angel

Paul Clark

Angel Grove Congregation in the late 1970's

Rev. G.D. Waits doing the Children's Story on Sunday Morning.
Rev. Waits started this program.

Choir

Angel Grove Choir in late 1970's
Rev. G.D. Waits, Int. Pastor, Alvin Stephenson, Director

Jimmy Wood

CHOIR
DIRECTORS

S.T. Moore
W.L. Andrews
Roy Couch
Curtis Johnson
Jimmy Gene Wood
Alvin Stephenson
Dee Ingram
Wayne Dozier

Alvin Stephenson who served
as Choir Director for 31 years.

Wayne Dozier

First Christmas Cantata 1981 "Carols by Candlelight"

Music

Sharon Shaw

Becky Craven has served as organist
of Angel Grove for 16 years and
is the present organist. She and
Jan Calhoun served as a team for
a number of years beginning when
they were 13 years old. Becky
has taught Sunday School, Training
Union, Mission Friends for a
number of years. She has also
been Vacation Bible School principal
and teacher. And has been in
charge of the Children's Christmas
Program.

Marilyn (Stephenson) O'Donnell

Jan Calhoun, served for a number
of years as our church pianist.
She and Becky Angel played piano
and organ. They started playing
at the age of 13.

Kay Hyde

68

Laura (Angel) Lockette

Nannie Sue (Angel) Stephenson

Lois (Wynn) Wilson

Ruth (Wynn) Hollingsworth

Ethel Angel

Celeste (Prickett) Johnson

Betty (Angel) Noah

Martha (Harris) Leonard

Peggy   Boozer

Daphnee
    Nunnally
    Connell

Doris (Angel) Calhoun

Mary Ann
    Haynie
    Picture
    Not
    Available

Brenda (Walker) Angel

Arry (Owens) Johnson

73

SUNDAY SCHOOL

In the 1888 minutes of the Tallasahatchee and Ten Island Baptist Association held at Rabbittown Baptist Church, Angel Grove Baptist Church, whose post office was Tampa, Alabama, reported 41 Sunday School members. Neither a Superintendent nor any officers were reported.

At this early time of our Sunday School, the church building was a one room wooden structure. Later curtains were placed and drawn to divide the building into classrooms.

The goals and purposes of Sunday School have continued through the years with blessings from our Lord. Quote from the Calhoun Baptist Association minutes, October, 1894, "It has been affirmed by wise men that the Sabbath-Schools are churches at work. They should be under the supervision of the church and the supreme object should be to teach the Word of God, that comes to us sealed with divinity, burdened with the theme of salvation and offers of everlasting life. The teachers and officers should be regenerated people. Sunday Schools bring the Word of God in contact with tender hearts. When children learn God's Word, we have hope that it will make them wise unto salvation" end of quote.

The first Sunday School Superintendent reported in October, 1894, was Paul Willington. Sunday School enrollment was 50 with 9 teachers and officers.

Other persons who served as Sunday School Superintendents are:

1895 - S.D. Kirby
1896 - W. T. Bridges
1897 - Wheeler Dillard
1900 - Ed Clark
1902 - J.F. Noah
1906 - G. W. Moore
1910 - D. M. Gardner
1911 - S. T. Moore
1913 - O.E. Vineyard
1914 - H. E. Wynn
1915 - S. T. Moore
1916 - H. E. Wynn
1921 - I. A. Clark
1923 - A. L. Weaver
1924 - Robert Wynn
1925 - Ed Moore
1926 - W. H. Angel
1929 - Roy W. Couch
1932 - Roscoe Wilson
1933 - Roscoe Wilson
1935 - Samuel Wilson
1939 - Clyde Brittain
1940 - J. M. Prickett
1948 - Roy W. Couch

JESUS, THE BREAD OF LIFE
John 6:26-51.
Golden Text: Jesus said unto them, I am the bread of life.
John 6:35.

Sunday School Card
First Quarter - 1908

1949 - Doyle Pritchett
1955 - Charles Calhoun
1958 - Eugene Angel
1960 - Edward Johnson
1973 - Doyle Pritchett
1974 - Don Carroll
1975 - Gene Johnson
1978 - Roscoe Angel
1979 - Rodney Young
1982 - William Miller
1983 - Rodney Young
1986 - Bill Denkins
1987 - Michael L. Johnson

JESUS HELPING A STRANGER

Sunday School Card
Second Quarter - 1933

The Sunday School has come to be recognized as the church's largest opportunity for evangelism. By 1955 the Sunday School enrollment had increased to 140. At this time the Sunday School sponsored Vacation Bible School with 85 enrolled. At present Angel Grove Sunday School enrollment is 196 including officers and teachers. The classes occupy individual classrooms within the educational brick building. The teachers and leaders have done much work to make their classrooms a pleasant and inviting place to teach the Word of God.

Sunday School literature and teaching aids are purchased from the Sunday School Board in Nashville, Tennessee and from the Baptist Book Store in Birmingham, Alabama.

The Bible is the Book we teach, Christ is the Savior we lift up.

E.J. Clark (left)
S.T. Moore (right)

H.E. WYNN

I.A. Clark

Ed Moore

Mike Johnson

W.H. Angel

Roy Couch

Don Carroll

Bill Denkins

Samuel Wilson

J.M. Prickett

Doyle Pritchett

Charles Calhoun

Eugene Angel

Gene Johnson

Roscoe Angel

Rodney Young

Bill Miller

77

Edd Johnson served Angel Grove
Baptist Church as Sunday School
Superintendent longer than any other
person. He served 13 years, from
1960 until 1973. He died in the midst
of his final term. During his years
of service, various classes were begun.
Some of Angel Grove's highest attendance
records were recorded during his tenure.
Edd Johnson was ordained to the Deacon
Board in 1959 and served until his
death.

Edd Johnson

RUTH CLASS

ADULT LADIES

HALLELUJAH CLASS

ADULT MEN

ADULT MEN

NEW BEGINNINGS CLASS

YOUNG ADULT CLASS

GRADES 10, 11, & 12

GRADES 7, 8, & 9

5th & 6th GRADERS

3rd & 4th GRADERS

1st & 2nd GRADERS

2 & 3 YEAR OLDS

4 & 5 YEAR OLDS

Mrs. Anne Cockley,   Church Secretary

Rev. Eugene Burgess in his study.

THE CENTENNIAL COMMITTEE
(front l-r) Anita Burns, Pat Miller, Geraldine
Prickett, Joyce Tillison, Tracy Pritchett
(back l-r) Becky Craven, Lawrence Burgess, Curtis
Johnson, Will S. Prickett, Dora Sue Angel

EASTER 1988

Missy Helms

Hunter Johnson

Aaron Anderson

Church Nursery.

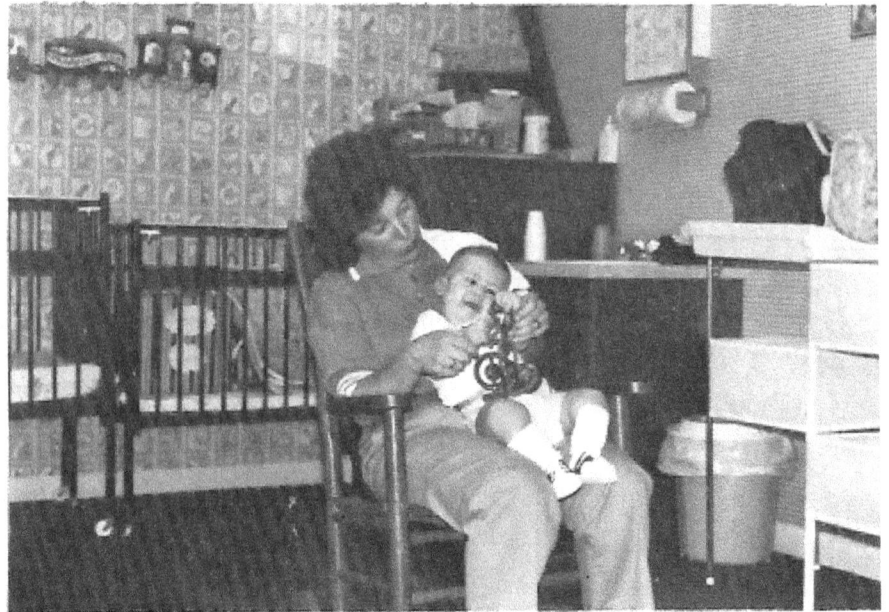

This is a picture of the
Church Nursery. Joy Carter
holding Todd Craven. Made in 1987

Church kids at Easter

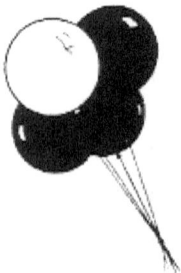

Church kids, Easter 1979

Easter 1971

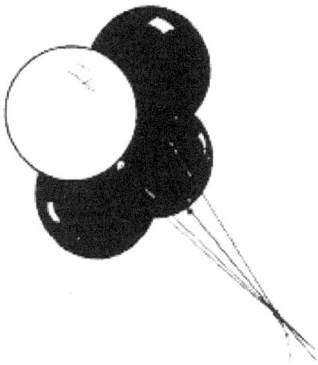

Church kids at

Easter Egg hunt - 1980's

Easter Egg Hunt in 1974.
This Easter was a wet and rainy
day, so it was held in the basement of Clytus Angel's home.

85

Adult Ladies S.S. Class in the 1960's. Left to right first row:
Mrs. Willie Segrest, Mrs. Willie Wilson, Mrs. Addie Angel,
Mrs. Mae Finley, Mrs. Ida Prickett, Mrs. Beulah Clark,
Back row: Mrs. Lucille Clark, Mrs. Ruby Pritchett, Mrs. Nella Wade,
Mrs. Annie Johnson, Mrs. Lou Hughes, Mrs. Annis McClendon.

Mrs. Trannie Owens Jr. Class
Doris Angel, Elizabeth Angel, Janet Angel, Mary Jo Wilson,
Alene Nunnally, Dora Sue Johnson and Mrs. Owens.

Mrs. Maggie Wynn's Sunday School Class.
Lila Mae Clark, Lucille Wynn, Florence Angel, Annie Clark,
Hazel Wilson, Frances McDuffie, Edna Clark, Nannie Mae Avans,
Louise Mooney, W.T. Johnson and Cecil Avans.

Sunday School Class 1927
Sue Nunnally, Trannie Couch, Ruth Wilson, Inez Nunnally
Lois Wynn and one unidentified.

Mrs. Alice Owens (card class)
Made at Sulpher Springs 1936-37.
Doris Robertson, John Henry Avans, Thomas Bryant, Bernice Angel,
Faye Bryant, William Carr, Lowell Bryant, Janet Clements, Judd Avans,
Elanor Angel, Betty Ruth Angel, Elton Couch, Vivian Angel.

Miss Alice Owens Sunday School Class
Marie Johnson, Bernice Angel, Betty Ruth Angel, Janet Clements
Elanor Angel, William Carr, Vivian Angel, Tracy Angel.

Ladies Sunday School Class
Left to right - Margaret Prickett, Sue Angel, Joan Bryant,
Nannie Sue Stephenson, Sara M. Johnson, Pauline Johnson,
Dorothy Hyde and Joyce Tillison

Sunday School Class

Mr. & Mrs. Ethel Angel's Intermediate
Sunday School class in the late 30's.
Left to right: Louise Angel, Doris
Angel, Dora Sue Johnson, Edna Simpson,
Elizabeth Angel, Mary Jo Wilson,
Nell rogers, Aline Nunnally, Mrs.
Ethel Angel, Elizabeth Robertson,
Edna Burgess, Janet Angel, Edna Angel.

Mr. Roy Couch's Sunday School Class
Vera Mullino, Eva Brittain, Mattie Lee Johnson, Johnnie Brittain
Ruth Wynn, Jack Hollingsworth, Rachel Wilson, Samuel Wilson,
Will Sam Nance. One girl and two boys are unidentified.

Mrs. Ethel Angel's Sunday School Class
Front row: Hazel Wilson, Frances
McDuffie, Lucille Wynn, Edna Angel,
Mary Anne Broughton, Nannie Mae Avans,
Audrey Dooley, Mrs. Ethel Angel,
Elizabeth Robertson, Edna Burgess.

BAPTIST YOUNG PEOPLES UNION

In the 1920's and 30's Angel Grove had an organization known as B.Y.P.U. which was Baptist Young Peoples Union. In those days preaching services were held only on the 4th Sunday of each month. Sunday School, and B.Y.P.U. met every Sunday, Sunday School in the morning and B.Y.P.U. at night. This continued off and on until 1952 when our first B.T.U. was organized. In B.Y.P.U. young people were trained how to serve the Lord better. It was a very dedicated and active group with adult leaders. Some of the early directors were:

```
1922 - H.E. Wynn
1925-26 - W. O. Vineyard
1928 - Gladys Kirkpatrick
1948 - Harold Smith
1949 - J. M. Prickett
1952-55 - Joe L. Johnson (first BTU)
1956-58 - Edd Johnson
1959-62 - Charles Calhoun
1963-66 - Arnold Johnson
1967-69 - Will S. Prickett
1970-71 - Roscoe Angel
1972 - Marshall Prickett
1973 - Mike Johnson
1974 - Doris Prickett
1975-79 - Lawrence Burgess
1980-81 - James Hobbs
1982-83 - Eddie Johnson
1984-85 - Jim Heathcock
1986-88 - Danny Craven
```

Harold Smith

Marshall Prickett

Jim Heathcock

Lawrence Burgess

Danny Craven

James Hobbs

Eddie Johnson

Arnold Johnson

ANGEL GROVE BROTHERHOOD

On December 12, 1970, a Brotherhood was re-organized at Angel Grove Baptist Church. Officers elected were: Director - Winston W. Wilson; Assistant Director - Charles Calhoun; Secretary-Treasurer - Will S. Prickett; Assistant Secretary-Treasurer - Lawrence Burgess; Program Director - D.D. Wade.

Members were: D.D. Wade, Roscoe Angel, Clytus Angel, Alvin Stephenson, Will S. Prickett, Lawrence Burgess, Winston Wilson, Charles Calhoun, Marion Clark, Doyle Pritchett, Dennis Boozer, Harold Littlejohn and Marshall Prickett.

SOME THINGS THE BROTHERHOOD HAS DONE

Installed waterline to the new pastorium; built a church sign; did work on the Fellowship Hall; gave food to need families at Thanksgiving, Christmas and other times; sponsored the R.A. program; gave out Bibles; helped keep the church grounds clean through work days; cut wood and did maintenance work for Senior Adults and others; helped with church additions and landscaping; planted an Azalea Cross on the hillside in front of the church; helped with the food and clothes closets.

The following men have served as directors:

1970-1971	Winston W. Wilson
1972	Marshall Prickett
1973-1979	Alvin Stephenson
1980	Donald Carroll
1981	Alvin Stephenson
1982	Jerry Haynie
1983	Eddie Johnson
1984	Lloyd Fike
1985	Bill Miller
1986-1987	Eddie Johnson

CARPENTER FOR CHRIST TRIPS

Coordinated by Ed Carter

Making the trip to Antwerp, Ohio were: Ed Carter, Will S. Prickett, Jackie Johnson, Sr. and Jackie Johnson, Jr. This trip was made with the First Baptist Church of Saks.

Our sleeping quarters in Antwerp, Ohio.

Before we began work on the church in Antwerp, Ohio.

After we finished hanging sheep rock and wiring in Antwerp, Ohio.

Making the trip to Albany, Oklahoma were: Eddie Johnson, Mike Brock, Jackie Johnson, Jr., Paul Clark, Jackie Johnson, Sr. Steven Hartsfield, Chris Johnson, Ed Carter, Jim Heathcock, Adam Heathcock and Will S. Prickett.

Scenic downtown Albany, Oklahoma.

The pastorium our men and boys worked on in Albany, Oklahoma.

Our boys, Chris Johnson, Adam Heathcock and Steven Hartsfield, made this catch for our supper.

Valentine Banquet in 1978
Doris Prickett is pictured. Doris
has been very active in Angel
Grove Church since her marriage
to Joel. She has served as the
WMU's Coordinator, teacher. The
first Youth Choir was organized
under her leadership.

Gloria Finley teaching
Mission Friends 1986

Becky Craven teaching
Mission Friends 1984

WOMEN'S MISSIONARY UNION

There has been a Baptist Women's Organization at Angel Grove since before 1964. In 1976, Acteens were lead by Judy Pritchett followed in 1977 by Doris Prickett, and later by Jeanette Johnson and Joy Carter.

In 1978, Mission Friends and Girls in Action were organized. There had been a GA organization at Angel previously.

In 1982 Doris Prickett became WMU Director following Anita Burns. In 1979 a Baptist Young Women's organization was begun under the direction of Pat Miller. At present there are 2 Mission Friends groups, 3 GA groups, 2 Acteen groups, a BYW, and a Baptist Women's organization.

In 1967 three girls from Angel Grove went to GA camp, in 1981 six girls, in 1982 12 girls, and in 1983 12 girls went.

G.A. and Acteen Recognition 1986

Acteen Coronation Service 1986

G.A. Campers 1982
Lori Schaller, Tessa Carroll, Lea Hyde, Andrea Cavender,
Melody Landers, Tanya Wigley, Tammy Weems, Kelly Fair, Shannon Brock,
Angie Jones, Cari Prickett and Stacy Rohershaw.

G.A. Campers in 1983
Melody Landers, Kandas Cavender, Andrea Cavender, Tanya Wigley,
Cari Prickett, Ali Williamon, Cristy Carter, Jennifer McKeachen,
Mia Lyn Pierce, Amy Young, Amy Carter, Shannon Brock.

99

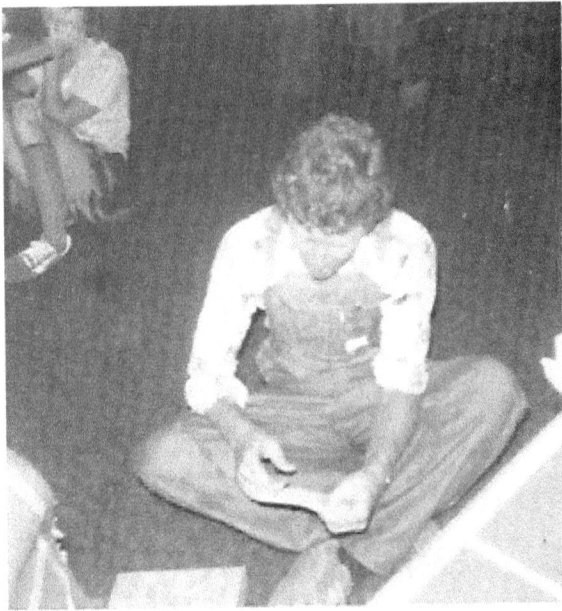

YOUTH
DIRECTORS

Allen Haynes
Tim Cochran
Doug Gregory
Gary Smith
Glenn Bonds
Paul Brown
Dee Ingram
Wayne Dozier
David and Sharon Shaw

Valentine Banquet 1977

Becky Angel

Marilyn Stephenson

Youth
Retreat
Group
1986

Group on Youth
Retreat in Florida
- 1986.

101

BALL Group

The BALL Group is an organization for, and is made up of, the senior citizens of Angel Grove and the surrounding community. It gets its name from its purpose - BALL - Be Active Live Longer.

The BALL Group was organized in the summer of 1985. This group had 23 members who chose their favorite scripture -- Phillipians 4:13, "I can do all things through Christ which strengthenth me," as their theme.

A luncheon meeting is held monthly, on the third Tuesday in the Angel Grove Fellowship Hall. Also, other social events, projects, and outings are enjoyed.

The group's first Directors were Brenda Fuller and Janice McLendon. Other 1985-86 officers were: President - Kathryn Putman; Secretary, Sarah Johnson; Treasurer, Lawrence Burgess; Devotional Leader, Carrial Crittenden; and Hospitality, Anita Burns.

1986-87 Directors were Joyce Tillison, Janice McClendon, and Joan Bryant.

1987-88 Directors are Joyce Tillison, Linda Bryant, and Inez Wynn. Other officers are: President, Lou Hughes; Secretary, Frankie Crittenden; Treasurer Kathryn Putman; Devotional Leaders, Carrial Crittenden and Doyle Pritchett; Hospitality, Anita Burns.

Through participation in group projects, each member is strengthened spiritually as well as physically and socially. Each project and event is planned that the Name of Jesus Christ will be honored and glorified.

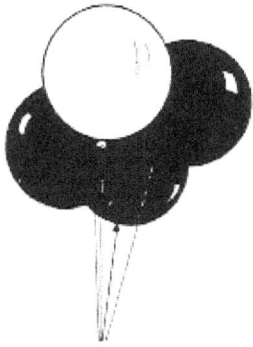

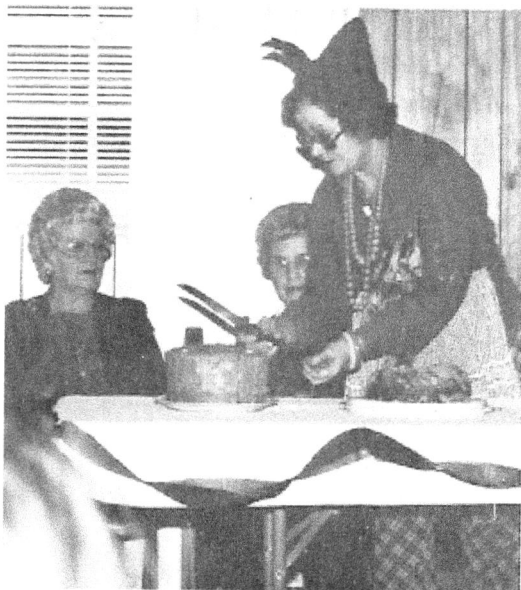

CHILDREN'S CHOIR

Children's Choir (ages pre-school-6th grade) began in 1976 in a Church Training class. The choir was actually formed in 1977, directed by Doris Prickett. Several cantatas and musicals were done by the choir.

In September of 1984 Beverly Landers began directing the choir. In 1985 the choir was divided into two choirs - pre-school and grades 1-6. Pre-school was directed by Gloria Finley, Becky Craven, and Linda Bryant. Grades 1-6 was directed by Beverly Landers, assisted at first by Carol Denkins and later by Susan Barrs.

Youth Choir Visits
the Museum, 1984

Children's Choir went

to the Nursing Home. 1978

Kasey Finley

Andy Craven

Mission Friends Group 1986

BUS MINISTRY

November 8, 1978, Angel Grove's Brotherhood appointed a committee to check on a church bus. This committee was Will Smith Prickett, Clytus Angel, and Marshall Prickett. On December 13, 1978, motion was made and passed by the Brotherhood to buy the first bus. Later, from the recommendation of the Brotherhood and vote of the church, a used bus was purchased. This first bus was bought on June 3, 1979.

In February of 1986, a committee was selected to get information about purchasing a new bus. This committee was James Johnson, Bill Miller, James Hobbs, and Danny Craven. Later this was put to vote and carried. A new bus was purchased May 23, 1986. A dedication of the new bus was held on a Sunday, May 25, 1986. In November of 1986, Angel decided to give Pleasant Valley Baptist Church the first bus they had purchased.

The bus ministry runs every Sunday morning for those who wish to ride. Angel Grove's bus minister is Brother Jackie Johnson. Others assist in driving on different occasions. The bus runs for Vacation Bible School and transportation to and from activities sponsored by the church.

Angel Grove's New Church Bus

Keys to the New Bus being delivered to the Bus Committee.
Bill Miller, Danny Craven, James Hobbs, James Johnson (1986)

By the Grace of God and the mechanical ability of Jackie Johnson and others, we at last, reached our destination of Panama City Beach, Florida for our youth retreat.

IN ONLY 12 HOURS!

Rev. Fred Curvin baptizing Joel Prickett

Rev. Hillrey Johnson baptizing Reese Jones, Larry Harrell and David Burgess.

TWINS -

Amy and

Sarah Ginn

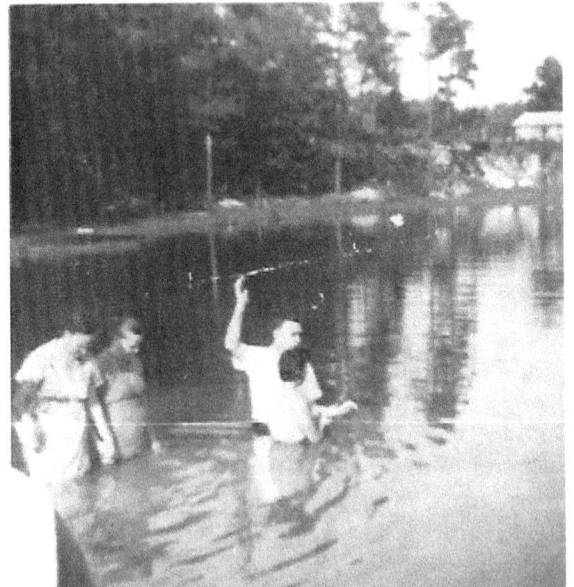

Rev. Walker Dean baptizing Geraldine Prickett in 1963.

Baptizing in creek in front of Jim Angel home.
Rev. W.H. Harris baptized the following: Ann Clark, Ivalene Miller, Jewel Clark, Louella Pritchett, Carolyn Wilson, Sherolyn Couch, Douglas Clark, Roscoe Angel, Bobby Hollingsworth, Julius Clark, Jimmy Wood and Judd Avans.

Rev. G.D. Waits baptizing in creek at Louis Hammonds.

Rev. Albert Bowman baptizing Paul Clark.

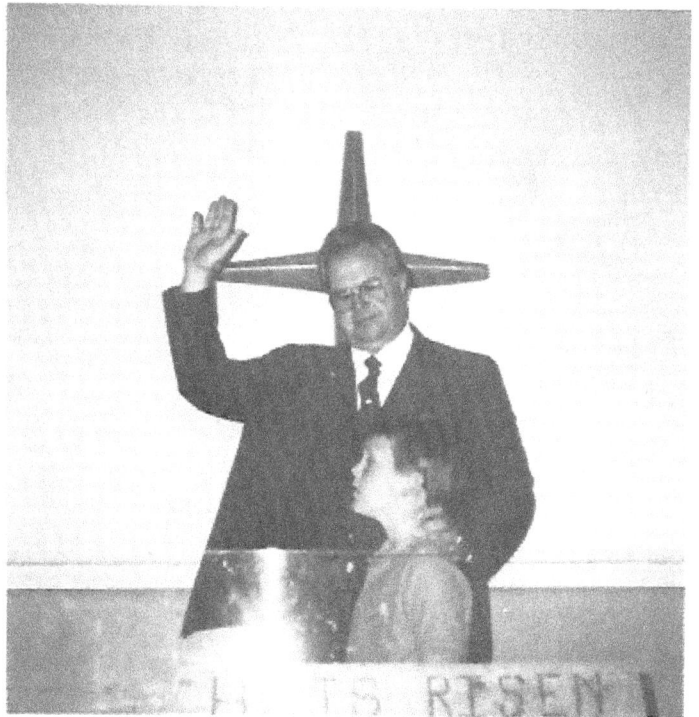

Rev. Eugene Burgess baptizing Andy Craven in 1988.

Angel Grove Had its first Bible School in 1952
when the Rev. Fred Curvin as Pastor. We have
had one every year since.

Vacation Bible School 1980's

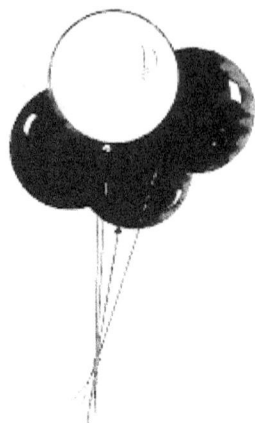

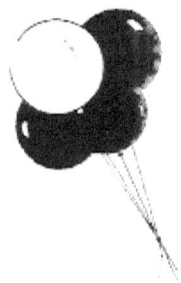

VACATION BIBLE SCHOOL

Bible School parade, June 1984

Bible School Kids in 1986

Please Come.

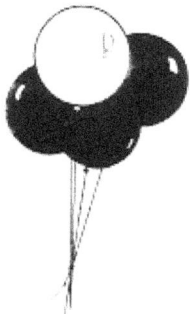

Bible School Kids 1986

Dedication of Angel's present Pastorium.
This was made in the early 70's. Front row left to right:
Roscoe Angel, Roger & Ricky Angel, Rev. D.D. Wade (pastor),
Alvin Stephenson, Kenneth Burgess, Clytus Angel (builder),
Stephen Pritchett, Stanley Pritchett. 2nd row: Joyce Tillison,
Nannie Sue Stephenson, Marilyn Stephenson, Gladys Angel, Douglas &
Tracy Pritchett, Doris Calhoun, Rev. C.C. McCain, Charles Calhoun,
Dorothy Burgess, Lawrence Burgess, Doris Prickett, Edna Burgess,
Edna Wilson, Dora Sue Angel and Jean Carter.

This is a group of Sr. Adult
Ladies made on Old Fashioned
Day in 1981. Left to right:
Mrs. Lucille Clark, Mrs. Beulah
Clark, Mrs. Ethel Angel, Mrs.
Effie Wood, Mrs. Annie Johnson,
Mrs. Ethel Carroll.

Old Fashioned Day 1982
Tanya Wigley, Kelly Fair,
Leah Hyde, Andy Craven.

Weddings

Mr. & Mrs. Danny Craven
(Becky Angel)
Married August 19, 1977
at Angel Grove Church
by Don Ledbetter

Mr. & Mrs. LaVern Barrs
(Susan Prickett)
Married Sunday, March 10, 1974
at Angel Grove Church
by Rev. D.D. Wade

Mr. & Mrs. Milan Robison
(Angie Wilson)
Married June 5, 1970
Angel Grove Church

Mr. & Mrs. John Klaustermeier
(Leah Knight)
married July 13, 1984
Angel Grove Church

Mr. & Mrs. Harold Lee Beauchamp
(Janna Brock)
married April 18, 1987
Angel Grove Church

115

Mr. & Mrs. Jerry Forrest
(Irene Lee) were
married March 9, 1974
Angel Grove Church

Mr. & Mrs. Randy O'Donnell
(Marilyn Stephenson)
Married September 10, 1983
Angel Grove Church

Mr. & Mrs. Tim Johnson   (Celeste Prickett)

Mr. & Mrs. Larry Worthy
(Velita Angel)
Married Feb. 9, 1968

Who was the person who said, "I'll always remember?" Mrs. Lou Hughes remembered when she and Reverend Hughes came to Angel there was a number of what she called "senior citizens," but most of them are gone now.

Orville Almaroad recalls walking up the railroad to the crossing (Couch crossing), then getting on the dusty road on his way to Angel Church. Mrs. Almaroad always brought a towel along in summer. This was to wash and dry feet at the creek (near Mrs. Angel's place), put on shoes, and be dressed completely then for church. On the way home from church the shoes came off again.

Mrs. Eunice (Burgess) Roberts remembers Tampi was a primitive Baptist Church erected at Seven Spring Cemetery. This church had been built before Angel Grove Church.

There were several singing schools and a commencement would be held at the school's closing. Students of the "singing school" would get up to lead songs that night or at that time. Some say they have never led another song publicly.

Mr. Clarence Bryant recalls in about 1926, it was a dry, dry summer. Rain was much needed. The church folk met, prayed for rain, it thundered, lightning, and began to rain before they left the church. He said the church was full, the altar was full. Mr. Tom Moore led the prayer for rain and Uncle Jim McKeown prayed. "You could see the teardrops falling from folks eyes," said Bryant.

Also, prayer meetings were held before services. The ladies met behind the church for their prayer meetings, and the menfolk went across the road, in a pasture, in front of the church.

Christmas time at Angel Grove was a good memory time with Martha Harris Leonard. Quotes from her newspaper clipping dated December 20, 1967, Birmingham News, says: "It doesn't take snow to make a perfect Christmas, not here at Angel Grove Church." She was four years of age when she took part in the spirit of Christmas here. Nearly everyone (goes) or went to the church, some early to decorate a Christmas tree and place gifts under it. Maybe a church class had exchanged names a few weeks before. Upon arriving at the church she says, 'You can hear the sound of a Christmas carol.' Mrs. Clytus Angel asks Martha, 'Honey, can't you sing, too?' Inside... In a few moments she says, 'I decided to be a piano player, too.'

Dark was approaching...Time to go back to Angel Church for the program. People met, hugged, maybe a hundred people or more. For an hour, singing carols was enjoyed, then the pastor did a short sermon, and then an outburst of oohs and aahs as the presents were exchanged. A lovely time...and a dear feeling for Tom Angel, who called Martha 'a real angel.'"

Martha was 19 years of age when the above story was written, looking forward to the night, at this age, of being at the program again. She was at the piano.

Martha Harris Leonard is the youngest daughter of Reverend and Mrs. Henry Harris of Angel Community, married to Jeff Leonard, two sons, Jeff Leonard and Judson Leonard. Martha is an accomplished pianist.

Christmas at Angel Grove
Mrs. Annie McDuffie is standing by tree. This is when we always had the tree on Christmas Eve and everyone exchanged gifts. This was a big occasion at Angel Grove.

Christmas Pageant 1959

Mrs. Annie McDuffie
A faithful worker, she always decorated the church at Christmas
and took care of the tree in years when this was a big event at Angel.

Christmas 1986

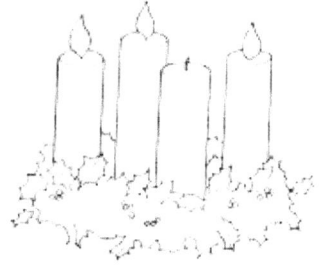

Christmas Season Events

PARTY

Young Adult Progressive
Supper - Christmas 1982

Valentine Banquet for Adults, 1987

Adult Training Union Social Dec. 1980
Alvin Stephenson, Clytus Angel, Alene & Robert Owens.

Halloween 1982. Ready to go
trick or treating on the bus.

Activities

WILLING WORKERS

In the fall of 1937, Mrs. Henry Harris talked to a group of ladies at the church about organizing a club and about projects to earn money for church activities. The club would promote a better religious spirit among members.

Interested members met at the church in the afternoon of October 27, 1937 to organize. The following officers were elected: President, Frances Bradley; Vice President, Mrs. Ethel Angel; Secretary and Treasurer, Mrs. Trannie Owens. The entertainment committee were Mrs. Annie McDuffie, Miss Annis Owens, Mrs. Bonnie Couch, and Mrs. Willie Angel. Other members were Miss Pearl Moore, Mrs. Annie Johnson, Mrs. Florence Boozer, Mrs. Ada Smith, Mrs. Effie Owens, Mrs. Willie Wilson, Miss Frances Wilson, Miss Geneva Couch, Mrs. Mag Couch, Mrs. Nancy Nunnally, Mrs. Inez Avans, Mrs. Bessie Angel, Mrs. Willie Harris, Miss Alice Owens, Miss Alma Wilson, Miss Ruth Wilson, Mrs. Addie Angel, Mrs. Clara Vinyard, and Mrs. Ruth Hollingsworth.

Members agreed to pay $ .05 membership dues and $ .02 at each meeting. The club's first project was that of making a quilt to be sold. It was decided that the members sell chances on the quilt at $ .05 each. On November 20, 1937, the club sponsored a concert by the Dunn Sisters at Cedar Springs School. Admission was $ .10 and $ .15. Food items were also sold. Bud Owens held the lucky number and won the quilt. After expenses were paid the club had a profit of $17.39.

On February 17, 1938, the Willing Workers Club made plans for a play to be given by the young people. Miss Ruth Wilson was given authority to order the play books. The play was presented on Friday night, April 8, 1938 at Cedar Springs School. A clipping from the daily newspaper reads:

Play To Be Given At Cedar Springs

A three-act comedy, "The Eighteen Carat Book," will be presented at Cedar Springs Friday night, the program beginning at 8 o'clock. Proceeds of the event will go for the benefit of the Angel Grove Church.

The play will be presented by members of the Willing Workers Club of the church. Among those who will take part are Frances McDuffie, Edna Angel, Frances Wilson, Bud Owens, Harold Smith, Frances Bradley, Lucille Wynn, Winston Wilson, Louise McDuffie, Buford Johnson, Ruth Wilson, and Curtis Johnson.

On April 14, 1938, the club voted to purchase song books for the church.

THE GENEVA "ANGEL" CLUB

On July 27, 1925, the newest organization of the Angel Community was the Geneva "Angel" Club. The first meeting was held at the home of Mrs. S.T. Moore and Miss Pearl Moore. Miss Geneva Couch, deaf and mute, was guest of honor. The purpose of forming the club was that everyone might learn the manual alphabet in order to communicate with Miss Couch. The club members would, also help and cheer the sick of the community. They would help with church work and plan other community projects. The Geneva "Angel" Club was called G.A.C. Girls.

Members of the club were Misses Pearl Moore, Geneva Couch, Annie Wynn, Trannie Couch, Ada Bowman, Audrey Avans, Flora Almaroad, Lois Almaroad, Clara Hopkins, Ruth Wynn, Rachel Wilson, Myrtle Reaves, and Nell Almaroad.

Each member was asked to pay $ .05 dues in order to finance planned projects. Donations of $ .42 and $ .75 were accepted on August 23, 1925 and on September 5, 1925, from the young men of Angel Community.

Lois Almaroad Burnham remembers winning a prize for best progress in sign language.

Geneva Couch (left) for whom the Club was named.

G.A.C. Club at Angel

Mr. & Mrs. S.T. Moore
sitting of front porch
of his store with
grandchildren, Edna
Moore Brown, Harold
T. Smith and Will Smith
Prickett.

Scene from Angel
Community at Moore
Home.

Home Place of Mr. & Mrs. I.A. Clark

Home of Mr. & Mrs. Willie Wilson.
After 1939 this was the home of Mr. & Mrs. Robert Johnson.

Mr. & Mrs. Tom Moore's Homeplace

Homeplace of Mr. & Mrs. Jim Angel. This house was
built at the turn of the century.

The home of the late
Mr. & Mrs. W.H. Angel

The home of the late Mrs. & Mrs. F.T. Angel

Former home of
Mr. & Mrs. A.L. Weaver
Presently the home of
Mr. & Mrs. Winston Wilson

The home of Mr. & Mrs.
E.J. Angel and family.
Formerly the R.J. Angel
homeplace, this home
was destroyed by a
tornado in 1954.

The home of the late Mr. & Mrs. Joe H. Wilson

Mrs. Maggie Wynn's

Home Place

Mrs. & Mrs. S.T. Moore
Early settlers in Angel Community and church

Mr. Tom Moore was a business man in the Angel Community after 1900, until his death in 1932. He owned and operated the first store and cotton gin, also operated a sawmill, farmed, and worked for the railroad. He, Mrs. Moore and several family members are buried in the Moore Cemetery in the Pleasant Valley Community.

In front of the old church at the foot of the hill in 1940.
Curtis Johnson, Wavel Couch, G.W. Angel, Henry Wynn, Jr.,
James Johnson, Robert Clark, Eugene Angel, Clytus Angel (behind hat)
Hearel Johnson (baby in arms).

Hog killing day on Edd Angel's Farm

W.H. Angel

Mr. F.T. Angel, sampling cotton.
He and his brother W.H. were in the ginning business for a
number of years.

Mr. & Mrs. Jim McKeown

Seven Springs School.
This school was close to the Angel Community across the road from
Seven Springs Cemetery. Mrs. Waters was a teacher there. Her son
Richard Waters was principal later at Cedar Springs.
This school was in existence until 1923. In later years it was the
home of Mr. & Mrs. Jimmy Johnson.

Home Demonstration Club in 1940's
Mrs. R.A. Owens, Mrs. Nancy Nunnally, Mrs. Louis Robertson,
Mrs. Effie Wood, Mrs. Addie Angel, Florence Boozer and Bernard
Elizabeth Johnson and daughter, Mrs. Etta Almaroad,
Mrs. Ruth Hollingsworth, Mrs. Trannie Owens, Miss Annis Owens.
One unidentified woman and child.

Mr. & Mrs. I.A. Clark

Rev. & Mrs. E.J. Clark

Mr. & Mrs. Jim Clark

132

Soldiers from Ft. McClellan at Angel Grove during WW II.
This is by the old church at the foot of the hill which was torn
down in 1947 when the present structure was built.

Old Store building run by Mr. Henry Bryant

Mrs. R.A. Owens and children. Early workers in Angel Grove.
All are deceased except Miss Alice and Ola, who are in the Nursing
Home. Left to right, Ola, Shelt, Arrie, John, Mrs. Owens, Robert,
Annis, Bud and Alice. Mr. Owens (the father) died at a young age.

For over 100 years the present school location has been a school
site for the Cedar Springs area. It received its name, so the
story goes, because a cedar tree grew in the spring.

About 1856 a long one-room frame building was constructed on
the present location. This site is located on lands in the SE¼
of Sct 7 and NE¼ of Sec. 18. T1rS R8E.

The six room frame building was completely destroyed by fire

.   The last Classes, Faculty & Workers (1987-88)
                at Cedar Springs School

            Children & Teachers from the Angel Community
                were a part of Cedar Springs School

The Calhoun County Board met in February 1988 and voted to close
Cedar Springs School at the end of 1987-88 school year.   June
3, 1988 will be the last day of school for the students at
Cedar Springs School.

HISTORY OF ANGEL COMMUNITY

Some early settlers of Tampi (or Tampa), now Angel, were J.W. Propse, A.J. Cross, Mr. Woodley, Mr. Elijhu West, Mr. David Woodall, S.J. Clark, and Mr. Dave Johnson.

Angel was the name given to the community around 1902. This was when the Seaboard Railway bought out the East and West Railroad, which was partially north of what is now Highway 204. Angel was named after Robert Jefferson Angel. He had operated a post office here when the community was called Tampi. The post office was located near where G.W. Angel's "Old Field Trailor Park" now is located.

ANGEL COMMUNITY BUSINESSES

Angel has had several businesses over the past century. Some that existed and, or still exist are:

1. Sawmill
2. Farming*
3. Ginning
4. Feed mill*
5. Post office (Tampa)
6. Builder's Coop, Angel Enterprise
7. Harte Industry (sewing plant)*
8. Towel outlet (Harte Industry)
9. Railroad Station-Depot
10. Hoodlum Train (Transportation train)
11. Bus from Jacksonville to Gadsden & return
12. Black Smith Shop
13. Horse Shoe Barn
14. Peddling Trucks - Rev. Lee Seibers - Rev. Emmett Boozer
    Harris Bryant
15. Canning Industry (supplied canned goods for Chastain Roberts Co.
16. Coal year
17. Cabinet Shop*
18. Dixie Clay Mine Industry*
19. Four grocery stores (one in existence now)*
20. Coso Upholstery Co.*
21. Cotton seed mill
22. Couch's Garage
23. Barber Shop
24. Grist Mill
25. Collie Nunnally Milk Sales
26. Charcoal Manufacturer
27. Bartise Mine

* Indicates existing businesses.

Old Train Station East and West Railroad.
Railroad who werved this area before the turn of the century.
Later the Seaboard Railroad was built. The area was known as Tampa
at this time.

People from all walks of life, with different talents and occupations have graced God's house at Angel Grove. Some were and are preachers, teachers, homemakers, post office employees, farmers, cattlemen, merchants, politicians, insurance people, secretaries, singers, musicians, soldiers, hairdressers, textile workers, home builders, telephone workers, nurses, mechanics, traders, saw millers, barbers, electricians, brick masons, sales people, seamstresses, Gideons, missionaries, truck drivers, foundry workers, railway employees, cotton ginners, doctors, bankers, and many others.

Some were visitors, some came and stayed, some were born and reared here in the community, some had folk who were at the beginning of Angel Grove.

Excitement, happiness, tragedy, sorrow. All these have been here just as at other places. We learn, we sorrow, we laugh, we praise God and say

TO GOD BE THE GLORY

May the grace of God and the love of Jesus Christ our Lord and the fellowship of the Holy Spirit rest and abide with us all now and forevermore.

AMEN

ARTICLES OF INCORPORATION

ANGEL GROVE BAPTIST CHURCH

STATE OF ALABAMA   *

CALHOUN COUNTY   *

The undersigned, Jim Heathcock, Paul Clark and Bill Miller, respectfully represent that they are the duly elected qualified trustees of the Angel Grove Baptist Church, Highway 204, Jacksonville, Alabama; That on to-wit: the __2nd__ day of __August__, 1987, at a special meeting of said church, the majority of the members thereof were present and voted and on said date and at said place, the following resolution was adopted, namely:

"Whereas, notice to the congregation was given on the __5th__ day of __July__, 1987, that on this date a resolution would be submitted to the congregation authorizing the trustees to be elected to proceed with the incorporation of the church, and in accordance with said notice, the following is hereby submitted to the congregation as required by law, namely:

Resolved by the members of the Angel Grove Baptist Church located on Highway 204, Jacksonville, Alabama, that the said church be incorporated as a religious organization in accordance with Title 10-4-20, Code of Alabama, 1975, et. seq.

Be it further resolved that three (3) Trustees be elected who shall be charged with the duty of completing the incorporation of the church as required by law."

The undersigned do further certify that the corporate name selected at said meeting is Angel Grove Baptist Church and that the undersigned were duly elected trustees for one year and until their successors are elected; that the object and purpose of said corporation shall be for the purpose of conducting religious services as provided by the Baptist Faith and shall have all the rights, powers and duties set forth and provided in Title 10-4-20, Code of Alabama, 1975, et. seq.

IN WITNESS WHEREOF, we have hereby set our hands and seals on this the _23rd_ day of October, 1987.

Jim Heathcock
Jim Heathcock

Paul Clark
Paul Clark

Bill Miller
Bill Miller

STATE OF ALABAMA   *

CALHOUN COUNTY   *   BOOK **46** PAGE **870**

I, the undersigned, a Notary Public in and for said State and County, hereby certify that Jim Heathcock, Paul Clark and Bill Miller, whose names as Trustees of Angel Grove Baptist Church, Highway 204, Jacksonville, Alabama, are signed to the foregoing instrument, and who are known to me, acknowledged before me on this day that, being informed of the contents of the instrument, they in their capacity as such Trustees, executed the same voluntarily on the day the same bears date.

Given under my hand and seal on the _23rd_ day of _October_, 1987.

Linda M. Kiker,
Notary Public

My Commission Exp. 8-13

139

BOOK **46** PAGE **871**

State of Alabama

Calhoun **County**

CERTIFICATE OF INCORPORATION
OF

ANGEL GROVE BAPTIST CHURCH

CALHOUN

The undersigned, as Judge of Probate of _____County, State of Alabama,

hereby certifies that duplicate originals of Articles of Incorporation for the incorporation of
ANGEL GROVE BAPTIST CHURCH
_____, duly signed

pursuant to the provisions of Section 64 of the Alabama Business Corporation Act, have been received in

this office and are found to conform to law.

ACCORDINGLY the undersigned, as such Judge of Probate, and by virtue of the authority vested

in him by law, hereby issues this Certificate of Incorporation of _____

ANGEL GROVE BAPTIST CHURCH
_____, and attaches

hereto a duplicate original of the Articles of Incorporation.

23rd

GIVEN Under My Hand and Official Seal on this the _____day of

December   87

_____,19_____.

Arthur C. Murray

Judge of Probate

'87 DEC 23 AM 11 29

LAST	FIRST	LAST	FIRST
ALEMAN	VICKIE	CARPENTER	LINDA
ALLEN	MARIAN	CARPENTER	ORIS La DON
ANDERSON	HUBERT LEE, JR.	CARROLL	DONALD
ANDERSON	MICHAEL	CARROLL	LESLIE
ANDERSON	SHEILA	CARROLL	LINDA
ANGEL	CLYTUS	CARROLL	MRS. ETHEL
ANGEL	DANNY WILLIAM	CARROLL	TESSA
ANGEL	DORA SUE	CARTER	AMY
ANGEL	DOT	CARTER	ARTHUR EDWARD
ANGEL	EDDIE JEFFERSON	CARTER	CHRISTY
ANGEL	G. W.	CARTER	JOY
ANGEL	GLADYS	CAVENDER	ANDREA
ANGEL	RANDALL	CAVENDER	KANDAS
ANGEL	RICKY NORMAN	CHRISTIAN	ROBIN
ANGEL	ROGER	CHRISTOPHER	BILLY EUGENE
ANGEL	ROSCOE	CHRISTOPHER	DANIEL MITCHELL
AVANS	CROLEY	CLARK	ALLISON
AVANS	MRS. ALMA	CLARK	ANDREW
BAKER	BRYAN	CLARK	ANNIE
BARRS	LaVERN	CLARK	BEULAH
BARRS	SUSAN	CLARK	CLIFFORD
BATEY	EULENE	CLARK	DAVID FRANKLIN
BATEY	HERBERT H.	CLARK	DAVID WAYNE
BENNETT	CORDEL	CLARK	JIMMY
BIBLE	LUCILLE	CLARK	PAUL
BOWMAN	CAROLYN	CLARK	RACHEL
BOWMAN	ELLIS C.	CLARK	ROBERT
BRITTAIN	NEAL	COLVIN	NAN
BROCK	JANNA D.	COUCH	BONNIE
BROCK	MIKE	COUCH	DAVID
BROCK	SHANNON	COUCH	GREG
BROCK	SHELBY	COUCH	JASON
BROUGHTON	MRS. LENA	COUCH	TONY
BROWN	DEBBIE H.	COUCH	WAVEL
BROWN	MRS. LILLIE	CRAVEN	ANDY
BROWN	PAUL	CRAVEN	BECKY
BRYANT	ERNIE	CRAVEN	DANNY
BRYANT	JOAN	CRITTENDEN	CARRIAL
BRYANT	LARRY	CRITTENDEN	FRANKIE
BRYANT	LENTON	CURTIS	JUDY
BRYANT	LINDA	DENKINS	CAROL
BRYANT	MELITA	DENKINS	WENDY
BRYANT	MOSES	DENKINS	WILLIAM
BURGESS	ANGELA	FAIR	KELLEY
BURGESS	ANNETTE	FETTERMAN	LINDA
BURGESS	BRAD	FIKE	LLOYD
BURGESS	DOROTHY	FIKE	LOIS
BURGESS	EDNA	FINK	SHIRLEY
BURGESS	KENNETH	FINK	TED
BURGESS	LAWRENCE	FINLEY	CASEY
BURGESS	REV. EUGENE	FINLEY	DAVID
BURGESS	SANDRA	FINLEY	GLORIA
BURKETT	KATHY	FORD	DEBBIE
BURNS	ANITA	FORREST	IRENE
BURNS	JENNIFER	FULLER	BRENDA
BURNS	JOHN C.	FULLER	FRANK
CALHOUN	DORIS	FULLER	KIM
CARPENTER	JOHN	FULLER	SESALEA
		GALAUDET	THERESA
		GARRETT	VALERIE

GAY	FRAN	KING	LINDA
GILMORE	BOB	KIRBY	MARY AVANS
GINN	AMY	KLAUSTERMEIR	LEAH
GINN	JONI	KNIGHT	JAMES F.,JR.
GINN	SARA	KNIGHT	JAMES, SR.
GORDON	CLYDE	KNIGHT	KATHLEEN
GORDON	MRS. CLYDE	KROLL	JERRI LYN
GOWENS	JANE	LANDERS	BEVERLY
GREER	CINDY	LANDERS	DONALD
GRIFFIN	PHYLLIS	LANDERS	MELISSA
HAYNES	EARL	LANDERS	MELODY
HEATHCOCK	ADAM	LYONS	LINDA GAYLE
HEATHCOCK	BELITA	LYONS	RONNIE
HEATHCOCK	HOLLY	MAGOUIRK	BARBARA
HEATHCOCK	JAMES	MAHONEY	CINDY
HEATHCOCK	ROBIN	MAHONEY	TOM
HELMS	MISSY	MANOR	NOVIE
HELMS	STEVE	MASHBURN	DAVID
HETHCOX	C. J.	MASHBURN	JEWEL
HETHCOX	WILLODENE	MEDLEY	RONNIE DALE
HICKMAN	REED	MILLER	ANGELA
HILL	ANN	MILLER	MICHAEL
HILL	EDDIE	MILLER	PATRICIA
HOBBS	JAMES	MILLER	WILLIAM C.
HOBBS	SANDRA	MILLER	WILLIAM J.
HOBBS	ZACH	MITCHELL	MARTHA JEAN
HOLBROOKS	ORVALENE	MORRIS	LUCILLE
HOOD	LELAN EUGENE, JR.	McCURLEY	MRS. MAUDE
HUDSON	MARCUS	McDUFFIE	JAMES RAY
HUGHES	MRS. LOWERY	McLENDON	JANICE
HULSEY	JERRI LYNN	McLENDON	STEPHEN
HYDE	JAMES	NOLAN	JANET
HYDE	MARY FRANCES	NOLAN	JASPER
HYDE	MARY LEA	O'DONNELL	MARILYN
INGRAM	L. D.	O'DONNELL	RANDY
JOHNSON	B. HEAREL	O'HARA	BEVERLY
JOHNSON	CHRISTOPHER	OWENS	ALENE
JOHNSON	CLAYTON	OWENS	DONNIE HAROLD
JOHNSON	CURTIS	OWENS	MERRILL
JOHNSON	DAWN	OWENS	OLA
JOHNSON	DONALD	OXYER	RICKIE
JOHNSON	EDDIE	OXYER	SHELLEY
JOHNSON	EUGENE	PARRIS	PAUL
JOHNSON	JACKIE	PAYNE	ALLISON
JOHNSON	JACKIE L.	PAYNE	CHERYL
JOHNSON	JAMES	PEARSON	JOYCE E.
JOHNSON	JEANETTE	PENTON	SHERRILL
JOHNSON	KATHRYN	PHILLIPS	KAREN
JOHNSON	KAY	PONDER	TONY
JOHNSON	MELINDA	PRICKETT	CARI
JOHNSON	MICHAEL	PRICKETT	DORIS
JOHNSON	MRS. PAULINE	PRICKETT	ELANOR
JOHNSON	SARA MARGARET	PRICKETT	FRANCES
JOHNSON	SHEILA	PRICKETT	GERALDINE
JOHNSON	SHERYL DIANE	PRICKETT	GROVER
JOHNSON	STEVIE A.	PRICKETT	GUY
JOHNSON	SUSAN	PRICKETT	JOEL
JOHNSON	VIVIAN L.	PRICKETT	LEOLA
JONES	ANGIE	PRICKETT	MARGARET
JONES	MELODY	PRICKETT	MARK

PRICKETT	MARSHALL	VOHUN	BRENT
PRICKETT	MICHAEL	VOHUN	ELLEN
PRICKETT	MICHAEL	VOHUN	FRANK
PRICKETT	RORY	WEBB	DEBORAH
PRICKETT	WILL SMITH	WEBB	DONNIE
PRICKETT	WILL SMITH, JR.	WEEMS	PENNY
PRITCHETT	BETH	WEEMS	TAMMY
PRITCHETT	COLEY	WHATLEY	FREIDA
PRITCHETT	JOEY	WHATLEY	JIMMY
PRITCHETT	JOHN	WHATLEY	KELLY
PRITCHETT	KELLY	WIGLEY	TANYA
PRITCHETT	KIM	WILBANKS	RONALD
PRITCHETT	PHILLIP	WILLIAMON	ALICIA
PRITCHETT	PHILLIP	WILLIAMON	BRENDA
PRITCHETT	SHEILA	WILLIAMON	JEANNIE
PRUETT	CLETHA	WILLIAMSON	LEDFORD
PUTMAN	KATHRYN	WILLIAMSON	MRS. LEDFORD
PUTMAN	LEAMON	WILSON	EDNA
PUTMAN	RICKEY LEE	WILSON	JERRE
RAINES	JUNE	WILSON	WINSTON
RAINES	STEVE C.	WOOD	GARY
RIGGAN	SHERRIE	WOOD	JANICE
ROBERTS	EUNICE	WOOD	LOWELL
ROBISON	MILAN	WOOD	WILBUR
ROBISON	PAT	WORTHY	VELITA
SATTERWHITE	TERESA	WYNN	HENRY, JR.
SAVARD	ALBERT G.	WYNN	INEZ
SAVARD	ALBERT G., JR.	WYNN	REBA
SAVARD	BETTY	YOUNG	AMY
SCHALLER	CYNTHIA	YOUNG	PAM
SCHALLER	GEORGE	YOUNG	RODNEY
SCHALLER	GEORGE, JR.		
SCHALLER	LORI		
SCHALLER	STEVEN		
SHARPTON	KAYLA		
SHARPTON	ROBERT	Angel Grove Church Roll	
SHAW	DAVID		
SHAW	SHARON		
SHEFFIELD	ARLON		
SHEFFIELD	SUSAN		
SMITH	CATHY		
SMITH	PATTY		
STEPHENSON	ALVIN		
STEPHENSON	ALVIN C., JR.		
STEPHENSON	NANNIE SUE		
STORMS	APRIL		
SULLIVAN	MERLIE		
SWANSON	DIXIE LYNN		
SWANSON	VINCENT		
THOMAS	DOLLY PAULINE		
THOMASON	JANIE		
TILLISON	BARRY		
TILLISON	MRS. JOYCE		
TOLLESON	RYAN		
TROTTER	ALLAN		
TROTTER	BARBARA		
TROTTER	SARAH		
VICE	ELOISE		
VINSON	ANN		
VINYARD	ARLICE